THE ASTR

2019

Horoscope Guide
& Planetary Planner

TAURUS

CREDITS

Contributing Editor: Suzanne Gerber
Copy Editors: Amy Anthony, Lisa M. Sundry

Cover Art & Zodiac Illustrations by The Grande Dame
www.grandedame.co.uk

Cover Design by Hortasar

ASTROSTYLE

Dedicated to the cherished memory of
Wendell the Love Dachshund (2000-18)

2019

A MESSAGE FROM
THE ASTROTWINS

Dear Astro-Friends,

It's been a heck of a ride here on this planet for the last few years, hasn't it? The world has grown more divided than ever—and it's left to the "lightworkers" and changemakers to deal with an existential dilemma. Do we speak up and fight, or are we only yelling into an echo chamber and fanning the flames of conflict? Do we refuse to "feed the dragon" and direct our energies to a higher vibration...or, by doing so, are we being complacent and complicit?

More than ever, we feel hashtag-blessed to have this extra set of divination tools that astrology gives us. Following the stars and planets might not reveal the *entire* story (that's where free will and human choice come in). But an extra layer of insight has helped make sense of some of the madness. Without astrology, we'd feel even more lost at sea!

Our resident numerologist, Felicia Bender, whose annual predictions we proudly include in every edition of this book, wrote in last year's guide about 2018 being a "master number" 11/2 Year. We all felt the paradoxical vibrations of the me-first "1" and the partnership-driven "2" in our lives. Here at Astrostyle, we expanded our staff and collaborated with amazing new people. But it was not without some growing pains.

In Chinese astrology (which we also include in this book), 2019 will be the Year of the Earth Pig. Although Pigs do like to roll around in the mud, they are also highly intelligent and sociable creatures that constantly communicate and cuddle with each other, sleeping nose-to-nose. After the last couple years, we could all use a cosmic group hug!

For 2019, the keyword is "integration." Jupiter, Saturn *and* Neptune will spend the entire year in their "home" signs—the zodiac signs that they rule—which will help stabilize the chaotic energy. And we're moving into a 3 Universal Year according to numerology, which is all about communication and creativity. Hopefully that will spark some productive dialogues and innovative solutions that stick.

The world is far from done with its tumultuous journey—which, we assume, will continue in *some* way for as long as the planet is spinning. But thanks to the stars, we can find some peace with it. For one thing, we're only midway through karmic Neptune's transformational sojourn through its native sign of Pisces (2012-24), a spiritually-awakening transit that happens every 164 years. Chaotic world politics, climate change and other modern crises are pushing the human race to wake up.

But we can't raise our collective vibration to a new frequency unless we get really clear that change starts with *us*. What will that look like in 2019?

Here's our road map for the year, designed to help you direct your energy consciously. How can you use *your* time, attention and resources most effectively? Let's plan it by the planets together.

Ophira & Tali
The AstroTwins

2019 # CONTENTS

MOONS, RETROGRADES + ECLIPSES

MAJOR TRENDS: THE OUTER PLANETS

THE 12 SIGNS IN 2019

NUMEROLOGY + CHINESE ASTROLOGY

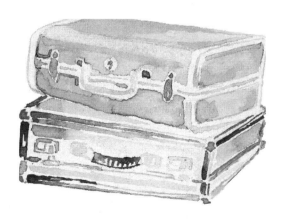

2019 FORECAST
What's in the Stars for All of Us?

Plant your soles on solid ground, but don't take your shoes off and get comfortable just yet. This year's cosmic lineup is an interesting mix of grounding earth-sign energies and motivating fire-sign mojo. After several intense years that have yanked our emotions all over the map, we need to stand firm—if only to regain our centers. But once we reconnect to our truths, it's time to mobilize!

Separation was a hallmark of 2018, which goes on record as one of the most divisive and polarizing years in recent history. With expansive Jupiter spending most of last year in Scorpio, the sign of extremes, it's no surprise. We were pushed to our most intense edges—and it was not easy. With super-sleuth Scorpio in charge, we saw sordid scandals and corruption exposed on a global stage. Things felt deeply karmic and unfair—if not outright confounding. How could this be happening? The rules we've been playing by for so long seemed to be suddenly null and void.

In 2019, hope might once again spring forth. Jupiter will travel through its native turf of Sagittarius until December 2, expanding our viewfinders from tunnel vision into wide-angle settings. With generous Jupiter in this free-spirited sign, we'll be able to see the bigger picture again, and take risks in the name of growth. Global ambassador Jupiter could usher in a more inclusive vibe, with space at the table for everyone. People might actually be nicer to each other, instead of ruthlessly looking out for number one.

We're no traditionalists—nor are we advocates of turning back the clock. But we'll be glad to see some of the timeless values of courtesy, mutual respect and compassion make a comeback this year. In 2019, Jupiter, Saturn, Uranus, Pluto *and* three eclipses will all land in earth signs at various points during the year. Earth energy brings stability and sensuality—it governs the material world. It reminds us to stay present and enjoy what we have.

But in high quantities, earth vibes can also keep us stuck or spinning our wheels. We'll need to make sure we don't get overly set in our ways. Materialism can also run rampant, as the sensory earth signs can get obsessed with accumulating "stuff"—something we don't need at a time when the world's carbon footprint keeps going up way too many shoe sizes.

 The AstroTwins' 2019 Planetary Planner

Luckily, Jupiter won't join this terrestrial tribe until December. Until then, the red-spotted giant will keep the visionary torch burning as he hangs out in fire-sign Sagittarius. Will this leave us with scorched earth... or simply warm us up for the hard work and tenacity that's ahead? Alas, we won't know until we put in the hours and pay our dues.

So...WWJD (What Would Jupiter Do)? In Sagittarius, he'd probably crank up the music, lay out a gourmet spread and turn this hustle into an adventurous party—complete with an open-door policy, a karaoke-friendly soundtrack and plenty of side-splitting jokes.

We'll RSVP "yes" to that, thanks! While many of the world's woes are no laughing matter, self-imposed suffering and seriousness don't ultimately serve anyone. As the stars bring us down to earth in 2019, we've got cosmic permission (make that marching orders) to find magic and mirth in the mundane moments. This year, the best thing we can do (in between fighting for justice, of course) is to relax and enjoy our short time on this earth—with hearts full of gratitude and a leftover case of the giggles.

That's how we can lighten the density of our spirits: by finding genuine pockets of joy, no matter what's going on around us. Only then can we start to transform the fear-based and stagnant energy that's overtaken this planet. By becoming the source of our own happiness, instead of waiting for the world to be "fixed" first, we reclaim our resilience. In fact, this ability might just become a 2019 superpower. Give it a try—the stars are standing at the ready!

> **"How can we lighten the density of our spirits? By finding genuine pockets of joy, no matter what's going on around us."**

Jupiter, Saturn and Neptune in their home signs.

This year, Jupiter will spend 11 months in its home sign of Sagittarius, ruler of global connections and cross-cultural alliances. Jupiter was last here for all of 1983 (the era of huge shoulder pads, Dynasty and Michael Jackson's King of Pop reign, then again in 2006-07, right before the real estate bubble burst. With magnifier Jupiter here, everything will go big and bold.

When a planet is in its "home" sign that means it's visiting the zodiac sign it rules, giving us a double-strength vibration of its energy. This isn't necessarily good or bad—it just means that whatever that force is, we'll experience twice as much of it.

Jupiter's outsized optimism, gregariousness and gambling urges will be matched by its counterpart—stern and structured Saturn, which is also in its home sign of Capricorn. While Jupiter pushes us to "go big or go home," Saturn will ride the brake, demanding that we plan, prepare and think of every worst-case scenario before we go leaping without a parachute.

How about we meditate on it? Spiritual Neptune is also in its home sign of Pisces from 2012 to 2024, continuing to fuel the fanaticism for crystals, astrology, meditation, and ritual that's swept through the world in the past seven years. We can expect more high-vibe hits from Neptune—but hey, we're not complaining. However, this double-strength download from the planet of illusion and self-deception warns against following false prophets and gurus. Looking for answers outside of ourselves, adopting a victim mentality and being utterly unrealistic? Yeah, that's Neptune in Pisces' handiwork, too.

Capricorn dominance: Will patriarchy win...or crumble?

The rooted energy of 2019 comes courtesy of three planets and three eclipses—with a heavy emphasis on Capricorn, the sign of structure, long-term goals and lasting traditions. Capricorn rules institutions, patriarchal society, men, government, big business, fathers and hierarchies. In other words, a lot of the "old school" stuff that people have been working tirelessly to reform and change over the past couple years.

It's been both painful and fascinating to watch. Last year, feminist reporter Hannah Rosin's book *The End of Men* tackles a new vision for the world where gender equality seeps into these outdated systems and institutions. The binary structure of us versus them, winners and losers, male versus female, haves and have nots, now seems hopelessly out of date. With the #MeToo, #TimesUp and #BlackLivesMatter movements accompanying a surge of social activism, feminism, transgender rights, and more—it's clear that we need to make this world

work for more than just a privileged few. Yet, a rise in right-wing nationalism reveals that many people feel threatened by this vision, and will go to extremes to resist a much-needed change.

But in 2019, resistance may be futile. Serious forces of change will be shaking these once solid foundations, even causing some of them to crumble. Structured Saturn and transformational Pluto will both spend all year in Capricorn, making their once-every-35-years conjunction (meetup) in late December. Expansive Jupiter will also move into Capricorn on December 2, pushing us to view old ways through a new lens. And in January, July and December, three eclipses in Capricorn could majorly overturn the way we work, live and conduct business.

Uranus in Taurus: A planet in its "fall."

Adding to the earth-sign cluster, changemaker Uranus will hunker into steady Taurus this March 6, staying until April 2026. This is the side-spinning planet's least favorite sign to visit, because they're such an energetic mismatch. For this reason, Uranus is said to be in "fall" in Taurus.

Uranus made a brief appearance here from May 15 to November 6, 2018, giving us a sneak preview of this tense negotiation. We're being asked to turn the tides without completely capsizing the ship—to make major changes, but not to throw the baby out with the bathwater. It won't be easy, as we'll feel the dueling demands between these cosmic forces.

 The AstroTwins' 2019 Planetary Planner

Chiron in Aries: Healing our self-image.

Reclaim your voice! As wounded healer Chiron, the comet that's now being given near-equal status as the planets, hunkers into individualistic Aries, we're all invited to heal any old pain around feeling invisible, silenced and ill-equipped to manifest our dreams. Naysaying jaws will drop as we scale new personal heights, shedding limiting beliefs and low self-esteem in the process.

Final Leo Eclipse: Leadership renewal?

Will the real leadership please stand up? Oh wait—that person might just be sitting in your chair. This January 21 will bring the final eclipse to ripple across the Leo/Aquarius axis. This series, which started back on February 10, 2017, has been largely responsible for the huge awakening of social justice and activism—as well as for the preening and ego-driven politicians who are pushing party lines instead of representing their constituents. From rallies to protests to demands for policy reform, the eclipses in #woke Aquarius, the sign of groups and humanitarian issues, have revealed the extremes of what can happen when people gather around a common agenda. This final eclipse—a total lunar eclipse and supermoon—will land in regal Leo, giving us one last chance to find our inner sense of dignified authority, and to express it in the world in whatever way, large or small, this feels appropriate.

Numerology: A 3 Universal Year

We're moving out of 2018's intense 11/2 Universal Year in numerology, which pulled us between the contrasts of individualistic "1" energy and the partnership-driven "2." From shifting alliances, selfish agendas and a desperately divided world, navigating that took a lot of inner strength. In 2019, we'll enter a 3 Universal Year, which is all about creativity and communication. Instead of shouting at each other, maybe we'll actually start devising some innovative ways of living that move us past the tired old models.

Chinese Astrology: Year of the Earth Pig

Move over, Rover. After chasing our tails in the Year of the Dog, the Earth Pig waddles in this February 2019. But don't get any "dirty" thoughts: Pigs may play in the mud, but they're some of the smartest and most socially advanced creatures—as well as serious cuddle-monsters! So let's get out of the dog house with its "best in show" competitions and start communing in the keep-it-real open pen. Sounds like hog heaven to us! ✳

NEW & FULL MOONS

Learn to manifest & motivate by the monthly lunar phases.

Following moon cycles is a great way to set goals and reap their benefits. Astrologers believe that our energy awakens at the new moon, then peaks two weeks later at the full moon. In many cultures, farmers have planted by the new moon and harvested by the full moon. Why not get a little lunar boost for your own life?

Every month, the new moon begins a two-week initiating phase that builds up to a full moon, when we reap what we've planted. There is a six-month buildup between new and full moons. Each new moon falls in a specific zodiac sign. Six months later, a full moon occurs in that same zodiac sign.

New moons mark beginnings and are the perfect time to kick off any new projects or idea. Lay the groundwork for what you want to manifest in the coming six months. Set intentions or initiate plans and tend to them for a half year.

Full moons are ideal times for completions, emotional outpourings, and reaping results. They're also your cue to cash in on anything you started at the corresponding new moon six months earlier. What have you been building toward? Full moons act as cosmic spotlights, illuminating what's been hidden. Take stock of your efforts and change course at the full moon. ✳

2019 New Moons

1/5	Capricorn (partial solar eclipse)	8:28pm
2/4	Aquarius	4:03pm
3/6	Pisces	11:03am
4/5	Aries	4:50am
5/4	Taurus	6:45am
6/3	Gemini	6:01am
7/2:	Cancer (total solar eclipse)	3:16pm
7/31	Leo	11:11pm
8/30	Virgo	6:37am
9/28	Libra	2:26pm
10/27	Scorpio	10:05am
11/26	Sagittarius	10:05am
12/26:	Capricorn (solar eclipse)	12:13am

2019 Full Moons

1/21	Leo (total lunar eclipse; supermoon)	12:16 am
2/19	Virgo	10:53am (supermoon)
3/20	Libra	9:42pm (0°) (supermoon)
4/19	Libra	7:12am (29°)
5/18	Scorpio	5:11pm
6/17	Sagittarius	4:30am
7/16:	Capricorn (partial lunar eclipse)	5:38pm
8/15	Aquarius	8:29am
9/14	Pisces	12:32am
10/13	Aries	5:07pm
11/12	Taurus	8:34am
12/12	Gemini	12:12am

Based on Eastern Standard Time (EST)

The AstroTwins' 2019 Planetary Planner

ECLIPSES

Expect the unexpected: solar and lunar eclipses bring sudden change.

Eclipses happen four to six times a year, bringing sudden changes and turning points to our lives. If you've been stuck in indecision about an issue, an eclipse forces you to act. Unexpected circumstances can arise and demand a radical change of plans.

Truths and secrets explode into the open. Things that aren't "meant to be" are swept away without notice. Shocking as their delivery can be, eclipses help open up space for the new.

The ancients used to hide from eclipses and viewed them as omens or bearers of disruptive change. And who could blame them? They planted, hunted, fished and moved by the cycles of nature and the stars. While the modern astrological approach is not fear-based, we must still respect the eclipses' power.

Solar vs. Lunar Eclipses

There are two types of eclipses—solar and lunar. Lunar eclipses fall at full moons. The earth passes directly between the Sun and the moon, cutting off their communication and casting a shadow on the earth, which often appears in dramatic red and brown shades. A solar eclipse takes place when the new moon passes between the Sun and the earth, shadowing the Sun. The effect is like a spiritual power outage—a solar eclipse either makes you feel wildly off-center, or your mind becomes crystal-clear.

The effects of an eclipse can usually be felt for three to five days before and after the event (some astrologers say eclipses can announce themselves a month before or after, too). Expect the unexpected, and wait for the dust to settle before you act on any eclipse-fueled impulses.
✳

2019 Eclipses

1/5: Capricorn (partial solar eclipse)

1/21: Leo (total lunar eclipse; supermoon)

7/2: Cancer (total solar eclipse)

7/16: Capricorn (partial lunar eclipse)

12/26: Capricorn (annular solar eclipse)

RETROGRADES

When planets go "backward," slowdowns and chaos can ensue.

You've heard the hype about retrogrades—but what are they, really? When a planet passes the Earth in its journey around the Sun, it's said to be going retrograde. From our vantage point on Earth, it is almost as if the planet is moving in reverse. This is an illusion, but it's a bit like two trains passing at different speeds—one appears to be going backward. When a planet goes retrograde (for a few weeks, or sometimes even months), everything that falls under its jurisdiction can go a bit haywire.

The most commonly discussed retrograde is Mercury retrograde, which happens 3-4 times a year. Mercury rules communication, travel and technology, and these transits are notorious for crashing computers, causing misunderstandings, delaying flights and even souring deals. Astrologers typically warn against traveling, buying new electronic gadgets or signing legally binding contracts during Mercury retrograde. However, all planets go retrograde at a certain point. Venus reverses course every 18 months; Mars, every two years. The outer planets—Jupiter, Saturn, Uranus, Neptune and Pluto—spend four to five months retrograde every year.

Survival tip: Think of the prefix "re-" when planning the best use of a retrograde. Review, reunite, reconnect, research. Retrogrades aren't the best times to begin something new, but they can be stellar phases for tying up loose ends or giving a stalled mission a second chance. ✴

2019 Retrograde Planets & Dates

MERCURY
March 5–28 (Pisces)
July 7–31 (Leo/Cancer)
October 31–Nov 20 (Scorpio)

JUPITER
April 10–August 11
(Sagittarius)

SATURN
April 29–September 18
(Capricorn)

URANUS
January 1–6 (Aries)
Aug 11, 2019–Jan 11, 2020
(Taurus)

NEPTUNE
June 21–November 27 (Pisces)

PLUTO
April 24–Oct 3 (Capricorn)

CHIRON
July 8–December 12 (Aries)

The AstroTwins' 2019 Planetary Planner

JUPITER IN SAGITTARIUS

Global connections ignite as Jupiter returns to its home sign from November 8, 2018, until December 2, 2019.

Globalism or bust! Nomadic Jupiter buzzes through its native sign of Sagittarius until December 2, 2019, making #CitizenOfTheWorld the year's most covetable hashtag. There couldn't be a better cosmic cycle for exploring distant corners of the Earth, making friends in far-flung places or visiting your ancestral homeland.

Ready, set, expand! Traveling and connecting cross-culturally.

If life got a little too insular while Jupiter was in private Scorpio from October 10, 2017, to November 8, 2018, then 2019 is the year to make up for lost time. Fire up the Voyager feature on Google Earth and plan a trip to a new city...maybe one that wasn't even on your radar. Set up Duolingo alerts and let the app help you get comfortable with foreign phrases. Engage in philosophical dialogue with people from different cultures and backgrounds. In the year ahead, new innovations such as high-speed planes and trains will shorten the distance between overseas neighbors.

Adventurous types might even live abroad during Jupiter's yearlong phase, or set up a *pied-a-terre* in a second zip code. And no, you don't have to quit your day job to pull that off. While Jupiter cruises through entrepreneurial Sagittarius, the concept of an "office without walls" could become a living reality for many. Companies may choose to hire independent contractors instead of full-time employees. Or, they may adopt a flexible policy, allowing staff to set up remote workstations at home or in a co-working facility.

No matter your GPS coordinates, this is a stellar year to start that kitchen-table side hustle or take your home-based venture into the global market. For those *not* looking to live abroad, global expansion may be as easy as clicking your mouse three times to put in a bid for that job with the Barcelona-based company...or sliding into that across-the-ocean cutie's DMs. Liberation and self-motivation are the name of the game!

Fun fact: The first iPhone was released during Jupiter's last tour of Sagittarius, in June 2007. It's predicted that more than five billion people will have mobile phones by the end of 2019. That's quite the sequel!

Is it time to diversify your romance portfolio? Many people may find themselves making unconventional choices about love or simply opening up to the full array of options before them. Boundless Sagittarians like bicultural beauty Zoe Kravitz and proudly pansexual Janelle Monae will continue to be icons in 2019. Cue Jupiter in Sagittarius' favorite hashtag: #LoveIsLoveIsLOVE.

Border Battles: Immigration and Diversity.

Of course, the "borderless" lifestyle remains, quite sadly, a privileged one in 2019. Native citizenship (read: being lucky enough to be born on the right plot of land) continues to determine who gets to wander freely around the world. The strict and often racially-motivated visa and immigration laws may be a byproduct of repressive Saturn's tour of Sagittarius, which lasted from December 23, 2014, until December 19, 2017. That three-year stronghold intensified much of the xenophobia and strained cultural relations we are dealing with at present. During that cycle, fear of the "other" was bolstered by world events, from refugee crises to border wall frenzies to terrorist bombings in major cities. Politicians around the world capitalized on these emotions and a fierce strain of nationalism emerged. (Interestingly, both "alt-right" nationalist Steve Bannon *and* modernizer Pope Francis are born under the sign of Sagittarius.)

In 2019, Jupiter in Sagittarius will have some cleanup work to do from Saturn's restrictive reign. In many ways, conservative Saturn effectively shut down the Archer's "we are the world" mindset. Can Jupiter in Sagittarius open up borders again, or will this 13-month cycle shine a high-wattage klieg light on the deep divisions that we humans need to repair?

In the best-case scenario, Jupiter in Sagittarius can be a time of cross-cultural harmony and rekindled diplomacy. When fear is not a barrier, our human instinct is to explore and expand. It was Sagittarius Mark Twain who said, "Travel is fatal to prejudice, bigotry, and narrow-mindedness."

Since Jupiter entered Sagittarius on November 8, 2018, the call to connect cross-culturally has definitely grown louder. If you're lucky enough to live in a diverse city, make a point of expanding your network to include people of different socio-economic backgrounds. Yes, this could take an extra effort, especially with hate crimes statistically rising in major cities since 2014. (You called the cops on her for *what*?!) As Jupiter in Sagittarius reminds us, we all share this planet, and need to learn how to work together.

On the flip side, the double impact of Jupiter in Sagittarius may stoke fanatical fires or increase political extremism and religious fundamentalism. When Jupiter toured Sagittarius in 1924, Ellis Island was closed as an entry port into the U.S. and The Immigration Act was passed, which dramatically limited the number of immigrants allowed into the country.

The AstroTwins' 2019 Planetary Planner

Jupiter in Sagittarius will force us to deal with the lingering divisiveness. The battle lines might be drawn based on culture—or they may dissolve completely as people unify across socio-economic barriers to create a working solution for all. We could see major political leaders rise and fall. During past Jupiter in Sagittarius transits, Gandhi and Yitzhak Rabin were murdered, the Dalai Lama fled Tibet while Margaret Thatcher and Fidel Castro took power. The Nixon Watergate scandal also played out while Jupiter was in Sagittarius during the early 1970s.

Jupiter and Sagittarius are also associated with the creation of law—after all, Jupiter, a.k.a. Zeus, was the god of all gods in Greek mythology. International trade agreements may be rewritten before the end of 2019, while we may see more revolutions in unstable nations, especially where the resources are kept in the hands of the privileged few. Sagittarius is a fire sign, and rising heat levels may be a driving force behind uprisings, as populations are forced to move around for survival needs like food and water. During Jupiter's last visit to Sagittarius, in 2007, a major drought in Australia caused wheat crop production to fail and prices to increase around the world. Of course, necessity has always been the mother of invention, and new industries may emerge as others dwindle.

Educate and Edu-tain.

High-minded Sagittarius also rules media, education, and philosophical thought. With self-publishing tools creating a golden age for authors, 2019 will be a renaissance for media makers, teachers and students. Want to lead your own workshop or develop an online course? Or maybe it's time to circulate that dystopian sci-fi novel that's been sitting, fully edited, on your hard drive. Try out tools like Udemy or Amazon Createspace and spread the knowledge.

College retention may also come into the spotlight while Jupiter is enrolled in Sagittarius University for most of 2019. With student debt reaching record levels in the U.S., the ivory tower is less of a "next logical step" for the country's high school graduates. The call for affordable education could become louder. Online accreditations and even charter universities may grow in enrollment as adventurous Jupiter pushes the envelope.

Not the bookish type? No problem. Since jovial Jupiter loves to *edu-tain* (educate + entertain), opt for experiential learning. Enroll in a yoga retreat—or circus school! Train for a marathon. Or gain a new skill with an immersion program. How about spending eight months literally getting your hands dirty at The Organic Farm School? Or take the ultimate challenge during this outspoken cycle and try a ten-day Vipassana silent meditation.

This quiet timeout can connect you with your most profound thoughts, and *after* that, you can fully unleash! Turn those ideas into a full-length album or diversity-training workshop...or some sort of teachable moment!

Speaking of global education, studies show that educating girls and women is the key to eradicating worldwide poverty. If you're looking for a worthwhile cause to get behind in 2019, may we suggest educational reform for girls? One in three girls is married before age 18 in developing nations, and pregnancy complications are the leading cause of death for girls age 15 to 19 worldwide. By contrast, when girls are educated, they can contribute to their economies, breaking the cycle of hunger and poverty. As self-sufficient citizens, they are less likely to contract diseases that ravage their communities and cause widespread deaths.

Ambassador Jupiter in Sagittarius could inspire art, music, comedy and eye-opening memes that give us a window into other worlds. While Jupiter was last here at the start of the 1970s, (Aries) Clive Campbell, aka Kool DJ Herc, put the poverty-stricken South Bronx on the map. Using two turntables to isolate the "breakbeat," he fathered modern-day hip-hop—a genre that, to this day, remains both a celebration of black culture and an oft-political megaphone for the African diaspora.

History repeats itself.

Jupiter only visits each sign every 12-13 years. The red-spotted planet's last tour of Sagittarius was from November 24, 2006, until December 18, 2007. Flip back in your calendar and have a look. What were you doing during that period last decade? You may see themes from that time in your life emerge once again. This is a time for letting adventure lead the way; for taking more risks in the name of expansion.

For Tali, 2007 marked her inaugural pilgrimage to Burning Man, an annual event in the Nevada desert that has "Jupiter in Sagittarius" written all over. Think: camping, utopian ideals, experimental communities living together, heady philosophical moments punctuated by childlike wonder and joy, and of course...fire! Burning Man turned out to be more than a lark. When Tali returned to Black Rock City, NV in 2008, she met her husband Cory in their shared camp, then moved from New York to Seattle and married at Burning Man in 2009. They've been going annually ever since; a meaningful and adventurous honeymoon sojourn, and a chance to collaborate creatively and innovatively as a pair.

So, get ready! The "wild gambles" that Jupiter in Sagittarius may churn up could manifest more than you bargained for. (Like, say, a spouse and a cross-country move.) With stakes *that* high, however, do look before you leap. The point is to jump into an exciting new realm—and land on your feet! ✳

The AstroTwins' 2019 Planetary Planner

JUPITER IN CAPRICORN

Calculated risks and growth within a structured plan? We'll navigate this paradox as daring Jupiter visits cautious Capricorn from December 2, 2019, until December 19, 2020.

Ask, believe...achieve! On December 2, 2019, jovial Jupiter soars to the top of the zodiac wheel, joining stalwart Saturn and power-obsessed Pluto in Capricorn until December 19, 2020. Clarify goals and map out those milestones! The groundswell of ambition that's been percolating since Jupiter's counterpart, Saturn, entered Capricorn in late 2017 could reach a fever pitch during this 12-month cycle. With Jupiter's foot on the accelerator, stalled missions will forge ahead. Competition could get fierce as we all find ourselves on a quest to become our best. And we're sure to see some unprecedented developments in government, economy and corporate policies—all realms over which Capricorn presides.

There *is* a catch here, though. Jupiter is in "fall" in Capricorn, its most challenging position on the zodiac wheel. Many of the red-spotted planet's free-flowing and inclusive traits are muffled in the sign of the Sea Goat. By nature, Jupiter wants to swing out and take a risk, while Capricorn can be sober and discerning. Jupiter says, "All are welcome!" while Capricorn wants to curate an elite crew. There will be moments throughout this yearlong cycle where we feel as if we are pumping the gas and riding the brake at the same time! Our

gambling instincts could miss the mark—or even lead to corrupt choices if we leap before we look. Conversely, we may become *so* risk averse that we get stuck in archaic traditions that stall progress.

Capricorn's perfectionistic tendencies can be amplified by Jupiter's beams. Even if you are sitting on a million-dollar idea, you may be hesitant to move forward after December 2. One of the key lessons of Jupiter in Capricorn? Learning how to fail faster and bounce back quicker. After all, "mistakes" are part of the process. At the same time, don't overdo it on the trial and error—not only will that be expensive, but you might waste precious time reinventing a pre-existing wheel.

Jupiter in masterful Capricorn is a prime time to work with pro-level mentors and experts who can help you map out sound strategies for long-term growth. Capricorn is the zodiac's structure junkie and architect; it doesn't create legends, it creates legacies, baby!

A green business boom.

Expansion and growth are the holy grails of the modern age. Normally, "can't stop, won't stop" Jupiter feels right at home in this wildly excessive mindset. But under earth-guardian Capricorn's watch, progress must be harnessed and directed. More isn't necessarily *more* during this transit. Jupiter in clean, green Capricorn wants us to evaluate our footprints and then assess the impact that our empires have on the environment.

With natural resources dwindling and our water systems becoming alarmingly polluted, Jupiter in earth-sign Capricorn is a clarion call for sustainable businesses. Clean energy, like solar and wind, could grow in popularity as residential solutions. Developments in hybrid and electric vehicles could take an unprecedented leap. Companies like Starbucks have already begun to ban plastic straws and many major cities like Seattle now charge for grocery bags and have implemented a paper-only policy.

Mega-retailer H&M has already enacted a textile recycling program, inviting customers to drop off their unwanted garments to be repurposed into everything from insulation to carpet padding. We expect more corporations to shift in this direction—if only in the interest of capturing the younger, environmentally aware market.

Ballers or bailers?

In financially savvy Capricorn, Jupiter can act as an abundance agent—or a giant magnifier of our economic state of affairs. Whatever Jupiter

touches, it expands. If you've been manifesting consciously, it may soon feel like someone poured Miracle-Gro on your balance sheet. Hello, baller! This is a golden era for business-savvy types. Is it time to step into being the CEO of your own company or to step into greater leadership at your day job? Jupiter in Capricorn will spur you on.

On the downside, the galactic gambler's tour of success-obsessed Capricorn can make some folks susceptible to get-rich-quick schemes. People who have taken shortcuts to the top could also be exposed—and forced to move way back on the game board. Jupiter in Capricorn may reveal corrupt corporate practices, forcing us to "vote with our dollars" by aligning with ethical companies. Executives may be forced to step down over scandals (most likely in the form of mismanagement of finances or HR violations), carving out a space for rising stars to settle on those thrones.

Jupiter's last visit to Capricorn—from December 18, 2007, to January 5, 2009—serves as a cautionary tale of what *not* to do in 2019-20. This marked a major moment for the global economy, and not in a good way. Like a stadium klieg light, Jupiter exposed the fault lines in the failed banking system as the Federal Reserve and U.S. government were forced to bail out financial institutions. The stock

 The AstroTwins' 2019 Planetary Planner

market crashed and Wall Street goliaths, including Goldman Sachs and Bear Stearns, fell to their knees. Taxpayers had to bail out U.S. mortgage companies Fannie Mae and Freddie Mac. The real estate market took a major hit; homes plunged in value and record numbers foreclosed—while others discovered, in late 2008, that their life savings had been stolen by Bernie Madoff's firm. The toll was *major*!

In 2008, while Jupiter was in Capricorn, the United States elected the first ever African American as President. One of Barack Obama's first tasks? To put an "economic stimulus plan" in place to repair the shattered financial state of the nation.

Will we be on the right side of history this time around? It's almost anyone's guess as alliances shift and trade wars erupt. Stabilizing the world economy may become mission critical in 2020—which might mean embracing Jupiter's globalist mindset and working closely with other nations to fortify the collective good.

A new men's movement?

Capricorn is the sign associated with the masculine gender. As high-minded Jupiter tours the cosmic boys' club, men will be called forth to "educate and elevate" themselves. While a handful of men, including the late Anthony Bourdain, were outspoken advocates for the #MeToo movement, many dudes have remained quiet, supporting the movement from the background. The idea that women's rights are human rights—not "simply" a feminist agenda—may gather steam while Jupiter is in Capricorn. Men speaking up and speaking out

for equality could become a widespread trend in late 2019. Our fingers are certainly crossed.

Simultaneously, the so-called patriarchy (also Capricorn's domain) could gather its own momentum. We may see more backlash from an entitled group of men who are afraid that sharing the power means losing "their" power. With controlling Pluto in Capricorn from 2008 to 2024 and rigid Saturn here from December 2017 until December 2019, fears have been provoked, causing people to cleave to conservative values.

As Jupiter enters the picture, that collective resistance to change might loosen up. We don't have to throw out the baby with the bathwater, but could we update some of those traditions, taking the best and leaving the rest? Since Jupiter is also the lawmaker, the new structures we invent between December 2, 2019, and December 19, 2020, could be taken to the high courts for legislation. Here's hoping dynamics truly evolve throughout all of our societal structures—instead of merely dissolving into a giant, cosmic arm-wrestling match. ✳

SATURN IN CAPRICORN

Structured Saturn roots into its home sign of Capricorn from December 19, 2017, until December 17, 2020. With potent Pluto also here, deep structural changes are ahead.

How stable is your base? In 2019, astro-architect Saturn will spend the second of three years in its home sign of Capricorn, inspecting for "structural flaws." Are you building your dreams in the most sensible way? Did you apply for the proper permits and pass the tests with flying colors? If not, oops! You may have to contend with penalties and aggravating do-overs before those blueprints can be sent to production.

Saturn returns to Capricorn every 28 to 30 years, staying for about three years each time. Its imprint on history is indelible, tearing down outmoded structures and revealing some of the worst corruptions among world leadership. Saturn was last in Capricorn from February 13 to June 9, 1988, and then November 11, 1988, to February 6, 1991. If you can remember back that far, you may see recurring themes.

Can the weak spots be fixed with a remodel or retrofit...or is this job a total teardown? Steel your resolve: If something needs to be repaired, a simple patch-up won't do in 2019.

There *is* a silver lining to this overwhelming rebuild. Since Saturn's in its element in Capricorn, we'll be primed to tackle outsized challenges, even if we have no clue where the ultimate solution lies. While 2018 exposed the metaphoric cracks in our systems, in 2019, we can begin the restructuring work. As harsh as Saturn's audits can be, they are ultimately supportive. The goal is to help us strengthen our foundations, so we can keep "up-zoning" our plans and providing sustenance for generations to come. Where will this hit the hardest? Both Saturn and Capricorn rule the following areas: authorities (such as heads of states and CEOs), corporations, governments, the economy, father figures and the "masculine" realm.

Body-wise, our bones and teeth are associated with this planet and zodiac sign—and it's fitting. The skeletal system literally holds up our bodies like the steel beams of a high-rise skyscraper. The bones and teeth take the longest to decompose, a metaphor for the legacy that both Saturn and Capricorn inspire us to leave behind. On that note, pump up your calcium intake in 2019, and incorporate more nondairy (and thus, easier on the planet) sources such as seeds (chia and poppy), dark leafy greens (kale, spinach and collard greens), beans and lentils.

The patriarchy also falls under Saturn in Capricorn's domain, which has been both maligned and strengthened in 2018. Part of the reason for that is because volcanic, domineering Pluto is also in Capricorn from 2008 to 2024, riding tandem through Capricorn during Saturn's entire voyage through this zodiac sign. Talk about a double whammy of intensity! With the confirmation of Brett Kavanaugh to the Supreme Court last fall, the majority-male GOP gained the most power over the U.S. government since the Great Depression.

In 2019, we may see more shenanigans from the "good old boys" and entitled "bro culture." And since Saturn also rules limits and restrictions, this is bound to create pushback from the gender equality movement. Women's rights groups will continue to mobilize, a la Linda Sarsour's historical Women's March and the #TimesUp effort which was ignited on January 1, 2018, just weeks after Saturn shifted into Capricorn. Employees will demand stronger protection policies—as hundreds of McDonalds workers did in October 2018, when they staged a strike to protest sexual harassment.

Men who embody the "divine masculine" may emerge as allies to women, raising the bar for male behavior in 2019. The battle is bound to be discouraging at times, given Saturn's slow evolution towards results. Willpower is a must!

By the same token, this cycle may continue to reveal the most egregious acts of sexism within corporations and governments. The polarizing revelations will continue to take down some men abusing their power while handing others a pass because of their privileged stations in society.

In earth sign Capricorn, Saturn's magnifying glass will scan for flaws in the foundation of leadership and large entities, including their environmental impact. As global temperatures and sea levels rise, we will be forced to deal with the deleterious impact that consumer culture has on the planet. While stubborn Saturn makes us struggle to change our "standard operating procedures," corporations may have no choice but to do things differently.

In 2019, savvy retailers should rethink the long-held strategy of "overstock the shelves." Given the massive amounts of textiles and uneaten grocery products sent to landfills each year, innovation seems imminent. Will VR kiosks to "try on" clothes replace the overstuffed racks? Could wider aisles, cooking demonstrations—and even food banks—become the new grocery store norm?

It's time for some reimagining, especially as customers become more eco-savvy and concerned with the fate of this third rock from the Sun. Customization and "on-demand" production may become *au courant*, even if that means waiting longer for the drones to drop packages on our doorsteps.

Saturn & Pluto in Capricorn: An Unsettling Match.

With transformational Pluto also in Capricorn from 2008 to 2024, there are seismic shifts going on beneath the surface, sort of like tectonic plates move before an earthquake. Powerful, controlling Pluto deals in secrets and hidden motives. This shadowy planet can expose corruption, or it can alchemize it, raising us to a higher spiritual vibration. Saturn demands integrity and creates breakdowns that force us to do the repair work. In many ways, these planetary players are opposites: Pluto rules the esoteric realm, while Saturn governs all that is tangible and concrete. This can also be like a metaphorical volcano rumbling beneath our feet, pushing us to face facts before a situation explodes.

Will Saturn shape Pluto's changes into reality or will their joint effort cause more destruction and greed? Saturn and Pluto travel in the same sign every 33 to 38 years. Historically, their union has recalibrated the global power dynamics. They were conjunct in October 1914, near the outbreak of World War I. In 1948, their close alliance in Leo coincided with Israel's formation and a redistribution of power in the Middle East. The 1982 Saturn-Pluto meetup, in balanced Libra, was a time of economic recession with the highest unemployment rate since the Great Depression (which, incidentally, took place during Saturn's 1929-32 visit to Capricorn).

As Saturn and Pluto make their way through Capricorn, we'll feel their joint impact in government, business and the economy. People will transform the way they work, conduct commerce and deal with hierarchies, perhaps forming their own micro-economies or self-regulating communities.

We're hoping the end result will be greater clarity and leaders who are truly "for the people." But we may not know fully until January 12, 2020, when these planetary players make an exact meetup (conjunction). From December 20, 2019 until February 5, 2020, they'll be in ultra-close connection, so expect to feel it then. We've already experienced the tremors leading up to this. In 2018, befuddling summits shifted global alliances. Meetings between the U.S. and long-sworn "enemies of state" such as Russia and North Korea created polarizing spectacles—and non-spectacles since, in true Plutonian fashion, most of the "negotiating" took place in total secrecy. Meanwhile, trade agreements came under fire between long-time allies and peaceful global alliances turned into jaw-dropping power struggles.

The upheaval has left some people feeling safer and others totally ungrounded. In 2019, Year Two of Saturn's tour of Capricorn, we may see the theatrics level off a bit as the taskmaster planet clamps down on Pluto's sneak attacks.

Saturn in Capricorn through history: Surprising twists.

To understand what Saturn in Capricorn could bring, it's helpful to review past eras for recurring themes. Saturn's prior visits to Capricorn have brought major "people versus the government" movements. Dictators have risen to power while others came crashing down. Saturn is the great cosmic teacher, and at its best, it can reveal

The AstroTwins' 2019 Planetary Planner

impressive leaders who rule with integrity, making historic diplomatic moves.

Powerful leaders protecting the people & environment.

Saturn was in Capricorn in the early 1900s, when U.S. President Teddy Roosevelt, famous for anti-trust laws and "trust-busting," took office. Roosevelt, whose face is carved into Mount Rushmore, was known as "the conservationist president" for his pioneering efforts to protect wildlife and public parks. After creating the United States Forest Service, he established 150 national forests and protected about 230 million acres of public land.

Since Saturn moved into earth-sign Capricorn on December 19, 2017, the U.S. has seen its largest rollback in protections of federal lands in the country's history. The U.S. Interior Secretary is working to legalize offshore drilling on the coastlines which have been battered by shifting weather patterns and rising sea levels. Here's hoping Roosevelt's legacy rises again—our planet literally depends on it.

Activism & Women's Suffrage.

Roosevelt was also a driving force behind the Progressive Movement of the early 20th century, which organized to combat problems created by industrialization, urbanization and government corruption. It was a Saturn in Capricorn crackdown on the waste, greed and excess of the Gilded Age. Corporate trusts, in cahoots with corrupt politicians, were targeted by the Progressive Movement, which pushed for fair wages and the eight-hour workday.

Prohibition, which outlawed alcohol, also rose during this conservative Saturn in Capricorn era.

Women's suffrage thrived during this period, as activists gathered and fought for the right to vote. It was a well-timed challenge to the patriarchy, as women demanded to be let into male-only institutions they'd been excluded from. The feminist ideal of the New Woman—a bicycle-riding, educated, independent figure—skyrocketed as Saturn entered Capricorn in the 20th century. In 2018-19, the hashtag heroines are bringing women together, such as Tarana Burke whose #MeToo movement was re-energized by Alyssa Milano just before Saturn entered Capricorn.

The Great Depression.

Saturn entered Capricorn in March 1929, briefly backing into Sagittarius from May until November of that year. That summer, the stock market peaked and began declining, due in part to the faltering agricultural economy, excessive bank loans and a proliferation of debt. On October 29, 1929, also known as Black Thursday, the stock market crashed. While Saturn returned to Capricorn from November 29, 1929, until February 1932, the Great Depression devastated the U.S. economy. By the time Saturn left this sign, stocks were only worth 20 percent of their 1929 value, nearly half of America's banks had failed and 30 percent of the workforce was unemployed.

While we are not predicting a market crash simply because Saturn is returning to Capricorn, there is an undeniable bubble, brought on in part by the euphoric early stage of tax cuts and breaks. But as the U.S. federal deficit rises as a result, the Federal

Reserve may be forced to elevate interest rates to keep inflation under control. Some financial analysts are predicting a forthcoming crash as early as 2019. While we wouldn't be so bold as to say this *will* happen, if Wall Street has shown us anything, it's that history repeats itself. Pro tip: If you're purchasing or refinancing property or taking out a loan, lock in lower, fixed interest rates fast!

Fidel Castro & the Cold War.

Saturn entered Capricorn once again on January 5, 1959. Four days prior, Fidel Castro ousted the Capricorn dictator Fulgencio Batista. Soon after, Russia and Cuba got cozy and the Cold War began, leading to a slew of embargos that were lifted by Barack Obama, then reimposed by Donald Trump. As Saturn was leaving Capricorn in 1961, John F. Kennedy, Jr. came to power and the Bay of Pigs invasion attempted and failed to remove Castro, who went on to become one of the longest ruling heads of state in history.

Gandhi's Passive Resistance movement.

While Saturn toured Capricorn in 1930, Mohandas Gandhi led the Salt March—one of the most famous examples of passive resistance *(satyagraha)*. For 50 years, salt manufacturing was controlled by a government monopoly. Although salt was easily procured from the sea, it was a crime for Indian citizens to make or get their own salt, because the government charged a tax on it. Gandhi encouraged citizens to refuse this tax by making their own salt or buying it from underground sellers. The 24-day, 240-mile Salt March ended at a beach when Gandhi picked up a handful of salt and

held it overhead as a symbol of peaceful protest. This passive resistance movement ultimately led to India's independence from British rule 17 years later. Can justice be obtained through peaceful activism in 2019? It's hard to say. But more than ever, we're seeing proof of Gandhi's words that, "An eye for an eye only ends up making the whole world blind."

Stalin's Collectivization: Socialism gone wrong.

In the Soviet Union, an inhumane attempt at government intervention during Saturn's transit through Capricorn led to one of history's worst atrocities. In the early 1930s, Joseph Stalin forced rural farmers to "collectivize" their land, agriculture and livestock, turning over all output to government control. This was touted as a modern miracle: The means of production would be "socialized" and removed from individual control, allowing (ostensibly) for more equal distribution of food. Many farmers protested through acts of sabotage: refusing to produce and harvest crops or even burning theirs. The more successful and rebellious farmers were shot, deported or put in horrific Gulag labor camps. Collectivism created such huge upheaval around food production that it led to the Soviet famine of 1932-33, which had a death toll of 5 to 10 million Ukrainians. Worse, Stalin withheld huge reserves of grain from the citizens that could have relieved the famine.

Since Saturn re-entered Capricorn, the tariffs and counter-tariffs imposed between the U.S. and Mexico, Canada, the E.U. and China have hit some farmers hard. Hardline immigration policies

 The AstroTwins' 2019 Planetary Planner

have also impacted many agricultural and livestock businesses who rely on migrant workers for labor.

Build bridges, not walls: Construction & deconstruction.

Saturn and Capricorn rule constructions and boundaries—including literal walls. The Berlin Wall was built during Saturn's visit to Capricorn in 1961 as a way of stopping Eastern Bloc emigration into Western Europe. This links back to the previous time Saturn was in Capricorn, as people were fleeing Soviet-style regimes created under Stalin's rule. History came full circle when Saturn returned to Capricorn from 1988-91. The Berlin Wall was opened in 1989, and its demolition was underway for the rest of this Saturn transit. As Saturn moves into Capricorn again, Donald Trump continues to press for a U.S.-Mexico border wall.

On a positive note, an architectural renaissance could be in order. Saturn in Capricorn can help us leave impressive (and positive) legacies that stand the test of time. Saturn rules buildings and architecture, and we may see some great new innovations in this arena, especially in the green and sustainable building genre. (Think: solar energy and living roofs for food production in urban areas.) While Saturn was in Capricorn from 1959-61, Frank Lloyd Wright finished the spectacular Guggenheim Museum, his last masterpiece before his death.

Saturn in Capricorn: Lessons moving forward.

How can we prevent troubling history from repeating itself as Saturn returns to Capricorn, placing a double dose of emphasis on systems, governments and authority? We must watch out for oppressive laws and ideologies masquerading as "revolutions." From North Korea's Kim Jong Un (a Capricorn) to Syria's Bashar Al Assad to Venezuela's Nicolas Maduro to Russia's Vladimir Putin, we are trekking through this Saturn in Capricorn cycle with perilous international leadership—and scary examples of patriarchal, authoritarian domination gone awry.

Since Saturn suppresses and Pluto transforms, this era might eventually put the kibosh on heavy-handed rulership and patriarchy. As Saturn clamps down on Capricorn's masculine rulership, we may see a rise in female government leaders and women business owners. Statistics show that educating girls and women is one of the vital keys to ending poverty. As women's participation in the workforce grows and conscious men help usher in the "divine masculine," gender roles will continue to be reformed. Here's hoping that men and women can work together in service of the planet's survival, uniting around the common cause of our shared humanity. ✷

URANUS IN TAURUS

The economy and tradition get an overhaul as Uranus enters Taurus from March 6, 2019, until April 26, 2026.

Snap your final duck-lipped selfies and binge-watch *Game of Thrones* (again). Until March 6, Uranus—the planet that rules technology and community—runs one last lap through Aries, the zodiac's "me first" warrior, before taking up residence in traditional Taurus again on March 6. Uranus only visits each zodiac sign every 84 years, electrifying the airwaves for about seven years and disrupting the status quo.

However, Uranus is in its "fall" in Taurus—a weakened position—since the energies are an awkward mismatch. Unconventional Uranus pushes for radical evolution and progress, while nostalgic Taurus roots into time-tested traditions, resisting change at every turn. Talk about an odd couple mashup!

We got our first taste of this seismic cultural shift last year. On May 15, 2018, the side-spinning planet poked its head into the Bull's pen, igniting a bizarre blend of avant-garde and old-fashioned energies. But due to its annual retrograde, Uranus backed into Aries on November 6, 2018, giving us one last round of the Ram's nearly eight-year tour of duty.

Uranus in Aries: Where we're coming from.

When combative, combustible Uranus first joined Aries' "fight club" on March 11, 2011, a magnitude 9.1 tsunami devastated much of Tokyo and caused an emergency in the nearby Fukushima nuclear plant. Shortly thereafter, storms erupted on the political front, beginning with the Arab Spring, then Occupy Wall Street in September of 2011. Throughout this entire Uranus cycle, marginalized groups have raised their voices in the name of inclusion and human rights. Uranus in Aries brought us the Black Lives Matter movement, the Marriage Equality Act, the Women's March, Transgender Awareness Week, and #TimesUp.

On the hotheaded flipside, Uranus in Aries also stirred a few frightening fringe uprisings, including ISIS and violent "alt-right" rallies. Autocratic rulers were emboldened, such as Russia's Vladmir Putin and his army of hackers, and Nicolas Maduro whose reign has caused a total economic collapse in Venezuela. Televised missiles were on military parade in North Korea. In the U.S., mass shootings (many in schools) have caused unthinkable grief, intensifying clashes between gun-rights activists and citizens like the students of Florida's Marjory Stoneman Douglas High School. And just as this cycle began with "fire and fury," it leaves acres of burned forests and islands devastated by hurricanes in its wake.

Television, which falls under Uranus' domain, has gone through a revolution since 2011. Behemoth networks lost market shares to indie productions from Amazon and Netflix, bringing us explosively popular shows like *Stranger Things* and *Orange Is the New Black.* YouTube stars are the new self-made celebrities, raking in major sponsorships and earnings that are not dependent on a Hollywood agent. The legacy of Uranus in Aries? Your shot at fame might just require a smartphone and a smile.

In many ways Uranus in Aries woke up the fighters in all of us. Activists found their voices, social justice warriors rallied for dramatic protests from airports to campuses to major cities. In true Aries fashion, there was even a tinge of "street theater" to some of these gatherings with flash mobs and props like pussy hats. In some cases, it felt more like a Roman Colosseum, complete with raw aggression, loud group chanting and torches.

While these outlets for collective rage have swung between jaw-dropping and cathartic, the question remains: Where is it all leading us? And what is it *really* going to take to create lasting change?

Uranus in Taurus: Where we're going now.

With Uranus in "brass tacks" Taurus, the revolution may be quieter, counting its wins in a newly quantifiable way. As the first of the earth signs, the Bull pulls our attention down to the level of the roots from which everything stems. To solve a crisis between 2019 and 2026, we will have to drill to the very base level (and preferably not with a fracking device).

> **"Uranus in sensible, profit-driven Taurus helps us monetize our creations in new ways."**

The Bull's motto is "lather, rinse, repeat." Between March 6, 2019, and April 26, 2026, a consistent effort will be required to ignite Uranus' revolutionary powers. We're betting that stamina will be tested, especially in this era of short attention spans. Instead of popping up for a weekend protest when something pisses us off, we will have to roll up our sleeves and get to work on the less "glamorous" stuff like reforming policies, attending city council meetings (over and over again), and organizing grassroots efforts.

When Uranus was in Taurus from 1850-59, Harriet Tubman became a major conductor of the Underground Railroad, risking her life through her quiet heroics as she helped to lead enslaved Africans to safety. In the spirit of rooted Taurus, it was literally an underground job, the quietest revolution that had an immensely profound impact.

Follow the money.

In recent years, the chasm between the "haves" and the "have-nots" has widened, as the middle class shrinks. Despite glowing economic reports of low unemployment rates and tax cuts, it remains to be seen if Wall Street will remain a bull market—even as Uranus cries, "Toro!" Interestingly, the Boston Tea Party took place during a previous Uranus in Taurus cycle, when demonstrators protested "taxation without representation." And the U.S. spent the entire last Uranus in Taurus transit climbing out of the Great Depression, which ended in 1941, right as Uranus departed from Taurus. President Roosevelt also signed the U.S. Social Security act, providing unemployment compensation and pensions for the elderly.

In Taurus, Uranus urges us to "follow the money" to discover who is *really* pulling the purse strings. Campaign finance reform may become a hot-button issue as citizens examine the way economic power has altered the political landscape—so much so that most modern-day government officials rely on outside funding to afford the high-dollar TV spots and other "publicity" required to keep pace with their contenders. As a result, their major donors may have as much of a sway as the constituents they represent. Will politicians reveal their funding sources or fight harder to keep their alliances under wraps? It remains to be seen.

Dollars go digital.

With technological Uranus in money-minded Taurus, mobile payment apps like Venmo and Apple Pay may continue to replace printed money. Self-checkouts are taking the place of live cashiers in many major retailers and cryptocurrency is still, well, cryptic to many and lucrative to others. Sensible Taurus could change the type of businesses that get funded. Rather than sink a load of venture capital into yet another social-sharing app, startup support may go to practical inventions that improve our daily lives. Of course, as A.I. replaces human labor, our relationship with money could go through a massive shift. Out of necessity, people may adopt the barter system, or take up the "gift economy" that's practiced at festivals like Burning Man. In this model, no cash changes hands, and goods or services are offered from a spirit of generosity.

The gig economy will continue to rise with indie-spirited Uranus in hardworking Taurus. More people will work remotely and in co-working spaces, and the full-time employment model may continue to wane. The Uranus in Aries cycle brought us opportunities to unshackle ourselves from the nine-to-five lifestyle, with solo venture options such as Airbnb, Lyft, and co-op offices like WeWork (and the all-women's space The Wing, one of our favorites!) gaining massive popularity. But there are also drawbacks, such as a lack of benefits and no actual ownership of assets. For the coming seven years, people may trend more toward owning a "share" of these places, perhaps receiving stock options in a company where they are independent contractors, or building equity instead of just getting a check.

> **"We may see scientific developments that revolutionize the farming industry."**

world may be totally transformed between now and 2026. An example of this is the world's food industry. The documentary *Wasted* pulls back the curtain, reporting that 40 percent of the world's edible production goes to waste—and 90 percent of the discarded food in the U.S. winds up in landfills. Meanwhile, approximately 800 million people on the planet are starving.

Uranus in sensible, profit-driven Taurus can help us monetize our creations in interesting new ways. Taurus rules the physical world and material objects. With freedom-seeking Uranus in sensual Taurus, we'll want to enjoy our possessions without being chained to them. While you'll be wise to downsize and accumulate less, financially-prudent Taurus still urges us to invest wisely for the long haul. Time to become savvier about saving, and discerning with our *dinero*.

With forward-thinking Uranus here, we may see scientific developments that improve soil quality, help growers and revolutionize the farming industry. Can we pioneer a solution to global hunger—one that doesn't involve factory farms and genetically modified seeds?

At this writing, scientists are developing 3D and 4D "printed" food that's actually edible. The saying "let food be thy medicine and medicine be thy food" doesn't only apply to your $15 chia seed pudding with young coconut meat. In 2017, scientists successfully transformed a spinach leaf into a working human heart muscle. With Uranus in Taurus, we may look to the earth beneath our feet, rather than the latest chemical concoction, to fight diseases.

Changes to farming and the food supply.

While Taurus is a creature of comfort, Uranus in this sign will challenge us to enjoy luxury without sacrificing sustainability. The very systems that have made modern life so convenient for the Western

The rise of populism and dictatorship.

The worst manifestations of Uranus in Taurus can be bigotry, stubbornness and warmongering. Adolf Hitler, a Taurus, seized power just as Uranus was ending its last transit of Aries, and retained his dictatorial grip through the 1930s, while Uranus was in Taurus. Mussolini also came into power during this last Uranus in Taurus transit, spreading fascism. As we enter the same cycle 84 years later, extreme right-wing candidates are once again on the rise, spinning propaganda through social media, slanted news outlets, populist rallies and cyber hacking. In the past few years, Uranus in Aries has provoked violent disruptors, many using technology to plot public acts of terrorism or to spread messages of hate. Hopefully, we will learn from history and not underestimate the "fringe" groups' ability to organize and gain critical mass.

From virtual reality to mixed reality.

Uranus in sensory Taurus will alter the way we interact with the physical and digital worlds. The VR world is developing ways to include smell, touch and taste from afar. Inventor Adrian David Cheok is spearheading the Mixed Reality Lab, which will engage all five senses in a simulated experience through "multisensory Internet communication." This Uranus phase could also take the IoT ("internet of things") beyond the smart house or driverless car. Perhaps we'll trade swiping and scrolling for device-free computing, as our digital gadgets become one with everyday household objects.

Arts & music: A digital revolution.

Time for some protest anthems—and new ways to raise consciousness? With Uranus in Taurus, ruler of the voice and throat, music could replace chanting and shouting. In 1939, Billie Holiday released her haunting "Strange Fruit," an anti-lynching song that reverberated through the airwaves. In 1935, Benny Goodman was the first Caucasian bandleader to hire an African-American musician to be part of his ensemble, beginning the "desegregation" of American music. Artists like Duke Ellington and Ella Fitzgerald (both Taureans!) rose to national fame, their songs helping to popularize—and in some states legalize—jazz.

Fine art, literature and dance will meet community activism and digital media (Uranus' domain), giving rise to stunning and quirky creations. In 2018, British street artist Banksy commanded $1.4 million dollars for the sale of his spray-paint-on-canvas "Girl with Balloon." Shortly after the Sotheby's auction closed, an alarm sounded and the painting began to slip below the frame, shredded by a hidden device operated by remote control. The half-deconstructed piece reportedly doubled in value *after* the partial self-destruction. That's what we call #UranianLogic! ✳

CHIRON IN ARIES

From wounded warriors to no-limits soldiers: Healer Chiron visits Aries from February 18, 2019, until April 14, 2027.

Oscar Wilde once quipped, "To love oneself is the beginning of a lifelong romance." But how many of us actually know what it means to truly *j'adore* me, myself and *moi*? For starters, cue the Whitney Houston and follow up with a Beyoncé-heavy playlist. The greatest love of all will soon be "happening to me" as Chiron—a comet known to astrologers as the "wounded healer"—began a nine-year journey through self-authorized Aries this past April 17, 2018.

According to Greek mythology, Chiron was a philosopher, teacher—and, yes, healer—who, ironically, could not heal himself. Chiron's placement in our natal charts, as well as its transits, can reveal a core wound that may take a lifetime to work through. But don't stress! Chiron is also a secret power. As you grapple with pain, you gain wisdom that you can pass on to others like a magical salve. In fact, the symbol for Chiron is shaped like a key since unlocking his powers opens up a portal to deep, inner peace.

Chiron orbits between two intensely oppositional planets—uptight, restrictive Saturn and liberated, revolutionary Uranus. His role as the metaphysical mediator can help us synthesize the energy of both. Where do we hold ourselves back (Saturn) and

CHIRON IN ARIES: TOUR DATES

Due to several retrogrades, the comet will weave in and out of Pisces and Taurus during this Ram-bunctious transit:

Apr 17, 2018	Aries
Sep 25, 2018	Retrogrades into Pisces
Feb 18, 2019	Aries
Jun 19, 2026	Taurus
Sep 17, 2026	Retrogrades into Aries
Apr 14, 2027	Taurus

where can we be destructively rebellious (Uranus)? We must understand both extremes in order to find the middle ground. In *Astrology and the Rising of Kundalini*, author Barbara Hand Clow refers to Chiron as the "rainbow bridge" between Saturn and Uranus. Aptly named, since integrating the full spectrum of emotions is the key to wholeness.

While Chiron generally stays in one zodiac sign for eight years, when he enters Saturn's orbit, he can buzz through a single sign in under two years. (It's up to him whether he wants to undergo outpatient surgery or opt for a longer course of therapy.) Since Chiron takes approximate 49 years to journey through all twelve zodiac signs, we all go through a "Chiron return" around age 50. At this point, core wounds may rear up for another round of cosmic therapy, especially if we've resisted doing any deeper self-examination.

Of course, there's always farther to go! Between ages 49-51, the Chiron return will certainly insist upon soul searching. If we've "done our work" we may be called into leadership roles that allow us to spread our wisdom and flex our healing gifts at this time. Chiron was last in Aries from 1968 to 1976.

Transiting Chiron sets the tone for universal healing: What wounds do we, as a world, need to deal with together? Take a look at Chiron's most recent journey through spiritual, esoteric Pisces—the water sign that rules healing and escape—that began in April 2010. The wellness movement is having a heyday now, from the popularity of juice bars and yoga studios to Oprah's *Super Soul Sunday* and guided meditations with Deepak Chopra. Shamanic healings, like ayahuasca and other sacred medicine ceremonies, are as prevalent in Brooklyn apartments as they are in Peruvian jungles. Whole Foods, once a boutique health food store, is now owned by the behemoth Amazon.

> **"Where do I belong? Do I even need or want to fit in?" We'll all be grappling with identity while Chiron transits Aries.**

Simultaneously, we are painfully present to the shadow of Chiron in Pisces, which also rules institutions like jails and hospitals, and governs our addictive tendencies. From privatized prisons to a distressed health care system to an opioid crisis, there are still wounds to be (ad)dressed! On a worldwide level, we'll all be grappling with identity while Chiron transits through Aries.

Where do I belong? Do I even need (or want!) to fit in? How can I maintain my individuality and *be part of a group?* If you're a Type A overachiever who can't leave the house without your brows on fleek and your outfit styled to Level: Paris Fashion Week, get ready for an existential crisis.

But don't freak out! It's long overdue. Before you can speed down the self-esteem superhighway you have to pass a toll booth guarded by your own inner critic. When the Snapchat filters are off, what voices come up in your head? Getting acquainted with your own self-deprecating thoughts is the way to neutralize them so you can replace them with empowering affirmations.

The AstroTwins' 2019 Planetary Planner

Warning bell: The goal of Chiron in Aries is not to achieve a narcissistic swagger of, "I'm a queen, get out of my way...I'm doing me!" Rather, think of the next nine years as a beautiful opportunity to understand (and love!) every voice that makes up the chorus of your personality. Are you going to let the tone-deaf-but-eager alto sing the solo aria during a performance at The Met? Heck no! But you're not going to kick them out of the choir, since you know that turning up the volume on other "singers" will integrate him into the composition that is you. In the sage words of Lao Tzu, "Because one accepts oneself, the whole world accepts him or her."

Interestingly, Chiron was originally classified as an asteroid but has gone through an identity crisis of his own. He's now considered a Centaur—part of a class of bodies orbiting between the asteroid belt and the Kuiper belt—and has been leveled up to "minor planet" status while simultaneously being categorized as a comet. Meanwhile, there are talks of calling him a dwarf planet, like his bro Pluto. But whatever his planetary pedigree, understanding his influence can be downright medicinal.

Rugged individualism, which has long been the mantra of the Western world, could hit its limit as oceans are polluted with plastic packaging, greenhouse gases threaten to melt the polar ice caps and the economic divide widens. While "Mine!" might be Aries' favorite word, Chiron in Aries will push for innovation instead of overconsumption. Rather than crowding racks with excessive merchandise, savvy retailers may soon allow shoppers to customize items on the spot through 3D printing and high-speed knitting machines that are gaining popularity in Japan.

Put down those VR and AR glasses—those are *so* Chiron in Aquarius and Pisces. The wounded healer's tour of physical Aries will make RR (reality-reality) en vogue! Instead of living vicariously through YouTubers, we anticipate a resurgence of live events like open-mic nights, interactive sports... or perhaps another upgrade to the Escape Rooms that Chiron in Pisces popularized.

The Ram is also an aggressive warrior, but with Chiron traversing this field, time's up on the "fight or flight" mentality. Drawing guns, dropping bombs, putting up our dukes...the world can't handle much more of that. Chiron in Aries is here to heal the "wounded masculine" which has fueled centuries of bloody destruction and devastation.

Simultaneously, Chiron in Aries may also reveal where a fear of conflict is keeping us stuck in self-destructive patterns. Yes, there's a time to fight for our rights—but is there a way to do so that doesn't involve domination, violence, one-upping and power-mongering? The inquiry begins! ✳

THE 12 SIGNS

ASTROTWINS

IN 2019

TAURUS

TAURUS

2019 HIGHLIGHTS

LOVE

Intimacy deepens as Jupiter plummets through Sagittarius and your eighth house of merging. With the adventurous planet in this sensual zone, it could be a sizzling year for communing—mind, body and soul. But you'll need to balance the no-limits bonding with "me time" as indie-spirited Uranus tears through Taurus and your first house of individual pursuits.

MONEY & CAREER

Welcome to innovation nation! With cutting-edge Uranus entering Taurus until 2026, one of your future-forward ideas could put your name on the map. You're a loyal workhorse, but it's time to speak up—and "up" your influencer status. With planets cruising through your ninth house of entrepreneurship and study, you may return to school or set the stage for launching an indie business.

HEALTH & WELLNESS

Fresh air and sunshine are your prescription for vitality in 2019. With a cosmic concentration in Capricorn and your adventurous ninth house, travel and wide-open spaces beckon. Get in touch with your outdoorsy side, from glamping to gardening to growing your own food. When you have a gorgeous vista taking your breath away (as opposed to getting treadmill-winded), you'll hardly even feel the burn. Love working out at home? Download your favorite instructor on YouTube. If you're feeling flush, invest in a Peloton for custom streaming workouts.

FAMILY & FRIENDS

A final Leo eclipse in January finishes a two-year renovation to your home and family sector. You may finally put down roots or complete that remodel. Meantime, eclipses in Cancer and Capricorn bring new friendships close to home and from afar. Travel and a fresh involvement in your neighborhood might garner new hotspots and homes-away-from-home.

The AstroTwins' 2019 Planetary Planner

TAURUS
2019 HOROSCOPE

2019 POWER DATES

TAURUS NEW MOON
May 4

TAURUS FULL MOON
November 12

SUN IN TAURUS
April 20–May 21

Shed some layers and prepare for reinvention, Taurus. 2019 could be one of the most transformational years of your lifetime—and we're not exaggerating. The cosmic lineup is launching your steadfast sign into highly experimental territory, while also pulling you into intense emotional depths. Neither of these are landscapes you traverse as much as you probably should. It's not that you don't want to, but your reigning role as the zodiac's provider keeps you landlocked in the material realm. Has fulfilling your day-to-day duties blocked your ability to dream and stretch beyond the familiar? *Boringgggg.*

Well, the stars have other plans now. Pack that caravan, call your electronic-music DJ friend and head to Tulum or Trancoso or Tanzania. Your "job" this year is to explore hidden corners and crevices of the globe, and to enrich your mind, body and soul. From swan-diving into sensuality to studying a fascination with the intensity of a PhD candidate, you'll crave experiences that stretch your perceptions.

With radical disruptor Uranus settling into Taurus this March until 2026, your first house of identity is getting a shakeup. Changes can come fast and without notice, which means thinking on your feet.

Check the mirror: You may no longer be the person you've always known. But that's not a bad thing. It will be disconcerting at moments, exhilarating at others. On days when you crave stability, your reliable anchors and touchpoints might be nowhere in sight. But be honest: You've felt change building momentum for the past few years, and now it's reaching a tipping point. That could bring relief, too. It's been like, Hey, universe, could you stop dropping all these weird hints and just point me in one direction already?

Constant adaptation is not the Taurus default setting—but once you get the moves down, you could learn to like this dance. And you'll have a great instructor! Methodical Saturn spends all year in Capricorn and your expansive ninth house, helping you integrate the changes through learning and mentorship. Ready to see how the other side lives? Saturn in your global and risk-taking ninth house can bring opportunities to travel, teach, study or start an indie business venture. A curious and nomadic spirit could become your new GPS.

But before you opt out of your day job and join the full-time festival circuit, there's some inner work ahead, too. Jupiter, the planet of growth and new adventures, is spending most of this year in Sagittarius and your intimate, transformational eighth house. You can't simply change the superficial parts of your life and call it a day. Jupiter will call you to look inward—deep into the shadows and unknown—and there may be some heavy emotional processing to do this year.

If you've always played the role of the "sensible one," delegate that duty to another zodiac sign. Between your spontaneous decisions to travel to Bali and the sudden urge to do "shadow integration therapy," there may not be much time left to tidy up the living room or plan the annual company picnic.

You'll be rewarded for your deep dive by the end of the year, as you blossom like a lotus bud (not to get cheesy on you, but it really could be that sweet!). On December 2, Jupiter will join Saturn in Capricorn and your global ninth house, pulling you out of the depths and into the wider world as 2019 draws to a close. If you're ready to share your gifts with the world—or to take the leap of faith and go big—the stars line up with their full support.

Uranus in Taurus: Radical reinvention.

March 6, 2019-April 26, 2026

As Greek philosopher Heraclitus said, "The only constant is change." Embracing this paradox will be your new M.O. for the next seven years, as radical disruptor Uranus settles into Taurus and your first house of self until 2026.

Uranus is in its "fall" when it visits your stability-seeking sign, meaning it's in its least comfortable position here. Prepare to learn the art of flexibility, even if it feels like a foreign language. As the zodiac's only fixed earth sign, you're the most grounded member of the zodiac, and this transit is as far from your natural inclinations as it gets. Not to get all Darwinian, but a species' survival does depend on its ability to adapt. Perhaps it's time to do some mystical mutation of your own!

You already sampled a taste of this new energy last year, when Uranus entered your sign from May 15 until November 6, 2018. The side-spinning planet sparked the urge to reinvent a part of your life or to blaze a solo trail. Since Uranus is the planet of surprises and sudden events, a lifestyle upheaval may have arrived out of the blue. Or, maybe you just felt a gentle but persistent rumbling beneath your feet, a knowing that change was coming.

Just as you were warming up, Uranus dipped back into Aries and your twelfth house of closure and healing from November 6, 2018 until March 6, 2019. Having a planet move from the secretive and flowy twelfth house into the highly visible and action-driven first house can be jarring, like waking up to a blaring alarm clock. And with Uranus going back and forth between these two disparate zones, your progress could have been abruptly stalled—or so it seemed!

If you veered down a side route or progress stalled while you attended to unfinished business, start your engines. The reinvention tour is going back on the road this March, as Uranus gallops back into Taurus on March 6 and remains here until April 2026.

With Uranus in your first house of appearances, don't be surprised if people start responding to you differently. The authenticity planet will make you more assertive and outspoken about your beliefs. You may literally wear them on your sleeve, marking your new identity with a tattoo or a bold new style.

Or, you'll just make some kind of 180-degree shift that leaves jaws on the floor.

Ophi's Taurus husband Jeffrey, an engineering-minded inventor who loves motorcycles and Formula One auto racing, suddenly took up yoga as Uranus moved into his sign last year. He literally picked up a mat and announced he was starting yoga at the studio across the street from his vaping supply shop. In short order, he became the only male student in a sea of serene middle-aged and retired women. Although he hasn't (yet) acquired a pair of hemp drawstring pants or referred to his classes as a "practice," Jeffrey claims it's quieted his busy mind and made him feel calmer as he prepared to send his daughter off to college. With hyperkinetic Uranus in your sign, a calming activity like yoga, meditation or just working out could help you stay sane when things feel chaotic.

If your birthday is between April 20 and 27, you'll feel Uranus' effect the most in 2019, as it will hover near the same degree as your Sun sign. Warning: When Uranus transits (moves) over your Sun, there can be uncertainty and changes that feel wildly out of your control. If possible, avoid making any hard-to-reverse moves now, such as buying a home, moving or a major relationship status change.

While you may get a wild hare to "rip the Band-Aid off" and go for it, the upset this can create could leave you sifting through rubble for months. Rebellious Uranus may tempt you to flaunt your independence, but taking an "I'll show you" attitude isn't a good enough reason to turn things upside down.

That said, if you're liberating yourself from an oppressive situation, proactive moves might be exactly what the cosmos ordered. Freedom fighter Uranus helps you recognize where you're tolerating subpar treatment or abuse. Daring Uranus in Taurus gives you the courage to make a swift exit. Your tenacious and loyal sign often sticks around long past the expiration date. Partly, you're afraid of change or you don't want to walk away from an "investment." But if all it's yielding is negativity and sadness, what have you got to lose?

Jupiter in Sagittarius:
Partnerships deepen.

November 8, 2018-December 2, 2019

All the way in…or all the way out? This year could take you to extremes, Taurus, as expansive Jupiter plunges into Sagittarius and your eighth house of intimacy, merging and shared resources until December 2. You'll crave more privacy and feel everything intently, as Jupiter magnifies your Spidey senses. During this focused year, you could get deeply engrossed in a project or relationship—perhaps to the point of obsession! At times, you may need to be pulled out of that all-consuming tunnel vision. But you'll feel so alive by letting yourself get swept up in your passion that you might as well go with it.

If you plug into to the right energetic channel, your power and influence can amplify. When Jupiter visits this realm, which happens only every 12 years, you feel everything so palpably it can almost be too much at times. Yet, you'll feel drawn to follow the strands of every mystery, which could evaporate maddeningly at moments, then pop up with another clue later. Keep connecting the dots, Bull, but know that the larger pattern will only reveal itself over time, with each stitch, each stroke of the brush, each soul-expanding risk you dare to take.

The eighth house is about investments—so whatever you put your energy into will eventually yield some kind of return. Be vigilant where you spend your time, resources and attention now. Whatever you plant will produce a bumper crop! Jupiter was last in Sagittarius from November 24, 2006 to December 18, 2007, so if you can, look back to those dates for clues of themes that can resurface.

Jupiter in this complex, layered zone is an intriguing contrast for you, because Taurus rules the material and physical realms, while the eighth house governs the "unseen." You may be taken so far out of your comfort zone you practically need a passport. Welcome to the holographic universe, where "living the dream" takes on a literal meaning. Embrace your role as astrological expat, and peek behind the thinned-out veil. There's so much you've taken for granted by operating on assumptions or always looking for definite answers. Riddles and paradoxes are the road to wisdom for you now.

The Greeks speak of two types of time, which they called Kronos and Kairos. Kronos (the root of "chronological") is linear time: plans, schedules, clocks, measured units of weeks and months and days. Kairos is that unstructured divine time—the place where serendipity and creativity and the Law of Attraction dwell. You'll go back and forth between these realms all year.

Last year, Jupiter traveled through your opposite sign of Scorpio, powering up your seventh house of committed relationships. This once-every-12-years transit took your closest partnerships to new levels. Perhaps you met someone who was the missing link in a business venture or who brought out a whole new side of you. With evolutionary Jupiter here, you can outgrow relationships—or at the very least, get really bored with the status quo.

Longtime couples may have reached a turning point, where your bond either needed an infusion of new experiences (travel, a move, learning new things) or you decided to part ways amicably. Some pairs experimented with role reversals: The breadwinner went back to school, the less structured partner became the "responsible one." The person who could barely be counted on to make a dinner reservation suddenly became the family travel agent and social director.

For single Bulls, global ambassador Jupiter may have sparked up a long-distance or cross-cultural connection that widened your perspective on, well, everything. It's common to meet a potential marriage partner with Jupiter here, and 2018 was a "make it official" year for commitments, breakups and contracts. You were called to take inventory of your relationships: Was there an even give-and-take, a mutual and harmonious balance? If not, Jupiter helped you explore new ways of getting back in sync or reworking the terms to suit you both.

This theme continues into 2019, but with Jupiter now in your eighth house of perma-bonding, the stakes are even higher. You'll want "all or nothing" under these intensified vibes, and the desire to go deeper emotionally, sexually and spiritually is practically a non-negotiable. Money matters will simmer with an equal intensity, and you could join forces with an influential person for mutual gain. Education-minded Jupiter sparks your curiosity, and you could matriculate on everything from tantric technique to human psychology to investing in cryptocurrency.

Has a relationship run its course? If you're still holding on like, well, a tenacious Taurus, Jupiter could pry your grip loose, possibly by putting a sizzling new person in your path. You're loyal to a fault and not likely to walk away from an "investment" unless you're 100 percent sure there won't be a decent ROI. Longtime couples might explore spirituality or attend therapy to dismantle any deeper blocks you've been avoiding. Bonds will be reinvented with Jupiter here.

As you courageously explore deeper emotional territory, it can be a bit of a roller coaster ride. But true intimacy, which is what you're after in 2019, demands this kind of vulnerability and honesty. Trust issues could rear up or you may have to have uncomfortable but authentic conversations about sexual desire and satisfaction. With revealing Jupiter in your eighth house of secrets, there might be a few rounds of "true confessions."

The eighth house rules power and the way we share our resources. Are you hoarding all your "toys" or are you putting a portion back in the communal pot? Are you playing the sole provider or are you allowing others to contribute their fair share? You'll want to be conscious of how you wield any newfound influence. Think of the infinity symbol, that continuous loop or "giving and receiving," as your guiding energy.

With lucky Jupiter in your eighth house of wealth, assets and passive income, this could be a "big money" year. Financial windfalls may arrive in large chunks, perhaps through a bonus, a real estate sale or an inheritance. You might take a gamble on an investment, and with Jupiter on your side, your risk tolerance increases tenfold. Pooling your resources with someone else could pay off, whether that means trying communal living or childcare or creating a joint business venture that allows you both to go bigger. Some Bulls may part ways from a longtime business or romantic partner, and this year could be about dividing up shared assets.

> **"With Jupiter in your eighth house of wealth, this could be a big money year."**

If you find yourself in an empire-building state of mind, important note: The spiritual eighth house reminds you that money is energy. The Law of Attraction is definitely on your side (so practice your "ask, believe, receive" skills), but it's not just about making a vision board or wishing on a star. The intention you put into this will inform what you'll get back. If you operate from fear and scarcity or greed, that will come back to you. It may be reflected in the way you feel around money (e.g., you make it but you can't enjoy it and never feel like you have enough). If you come from a place of love and abundance, you'll attract financial experiences that are aligned with that. Consider donating a portion of proceeds to a cause you care about. If you, for example, build a new home, check the ethical and sustainable business practices of the contractors. Sure, it may be extra work on the front end, but the sayings "as above, so below" and "as within, so without," have never been truer.

Reminder, too, that you're living in the holographic universe this year, and it operates on a different kind of timing. Yes, you'll get back what you put into things—but maybe not in the exact form and way you expect. Doing anything with an agenda or trying to force an outcome could lead to more painful lessons than anything. Investments require not only risk but also faith. And with high-minded Jupiter here, you'll need to learn how to remain trusting and tuned in when things don't follow a linear path or pay off instantly.

Developing your spiritual muscles will make all the difference during this Jupiter phase, as you might experience the gamut of life cycles, from births to deaths (literal or symbolic) and will need to be resilient. This is a time for dismantling emotional blocks and opening up to divine guidance. Some Bulls could have a major awakening now. You may crave more privacy and time to research and reflect. There's a strong pull to the metaphysical. You want to understand the meaning of life and death, or to explore mysteries of the human psyche and experience. This could be a time of emotional healing and discovery.

The people you're around could play a major hand in this, especially during three intense squares (90-degree angles of tension) between expansive

Jupiter and doe-eyed Neptune, which is in Pisces and your eleventh house of groups. If you've been gullible or too easily charmed by the people you're around, you may get a wakeup call during the three exact Jupiter-Neptune squares on January 13, June 16 and September 21. On a positive note, your openness could attract some amazing new friends, people who understand you on a deep soul level and open your eyes to a mind-blowing new perspective.

Rose-colored glasses alert: Make sure that, as you explore new financial endeavors or sexual awakenings, you don't fall under the Neptunian spell of a guru figure. While opening yourself up to teachers is important, a master manipulator in your midst might pull you into a cult-like trance. No human being has all the answers—and while guidance can be helpful, you'll want to seek truth within yourself, not from a charismatic outsider. Be vigilant about protecting your privacy, especially online.

The Jupiter-Neptune squares can make you vulnerable to identity thefts or "catfishing" schemes. If you're feeling overwhelmed by the intensity of 2019, these dates could be perfect for unplugging and going off the grid, perhaps on a vision quest or to an escape near water where you can regenerate and have a few deep epiphanies about life.

Jupiter in Capricorn: Stretching your limits.

December 2, 2019-December 19, 2020

Have whim, will travel! The end of 2019 puts you in full nomad mode, as wanderlusting Jupiter begins a one-year bohemian jaunt through Sagittarius and your ninth house of expansion, the higher mind and adventure. This is a unique moment in the cosmos, as structured Saturn and transformational Pluto are also in Capricorn (Saturn on and off until December 2020 and Pluto until 2024)—and December will also bring a galvanizing solar eclipse in Capricorn.

If you don't have your bags packed for a New Year's Eve vacation—or plans to host an otherworldly feast to fete in 2020—get busy. Decadent Jupiter rules the ninth house, so you'll get a double dose of hedonistic and caution-to-the-wind vibes for the next 12 months. While Saturn can restrain your appetite a bit, it also adds clout and stamina.

One of your wilder ideas may actually gain traction, even if it seems like "too much." If you're dreaming of going big, you'll have the follow-through to turn your visions into reality. Strike the word "impossible" from your vocabulary—it has no place there now.

Jupiter was last in Capricorn from December 18, 2007 to January 5, 2009. Look back to those times: Did you take any major risks or widen your perspective? With Jupiter in this growth-driven sector once again, you could travel, return to school, launch an indie business venture or swing far outside your comfort zone. You may be drawn to metaphysical topics or a search for higher wisdom. As you make your resolutions, think big. Jupiter in this no-limits zone will stretch your perceptions of what's possible!

Saturn in Capricorn:
Expanding and contracting.

December 19, 2017-December 17, 2020

The theme of balancing structure and freedom is a repeating pattern that's woven all over 2019 for you, Taurus. Just like irrepressible Uranus in steadfast Taurus presents this paradox, so too does structured Saturn, which is spending the full year in Capricorn and your ninth house of risk, adventure and major growth. Being daring and discerning all at once will be your challenge with Saturn in Capricorn.

Saturn began journeying through Capricorn on December 19, 2017, and it will complete its journey on December 17, 2020. You hosted Saturn here for all of 2018, and this year is a continuation of your quest for knowledge, truth and your highest purpose. Since Saturn is in a compatible fellow earth sign, it will form a flowing trine (120-degree angle of harmony) to your Taurus Sun. This can be a powerful year for taking decisive action around your dreams. Bulls born between May 3 and 11 will feel Saturn's authoritative influence the most in 2019.

Still, there's a paradox to navigate, because Saturn restricts and the ninth house expands. How can they settle this difference? Think of the ways that structure can set you free. Visualize yourself building a solid container, one that's designed to hold your dreams. After all, a vision that has no plan or direction won't manifest into tangible form—something any Taurus worth their salt knows. The

trick is not to suppress your ideas or stifle your creative process. Respect it and give it room to breathe. Allow space for blue-sky visioning before you start asking things like, "How will I monetize that?" or "When can I quit my day job and do this full time?" But don't let your Id run willy-nilly like a child on a sugar high. Otherwise, you'll just end up scattering your energy and burning out fast.

Think of cautious Saturn as a yellow light, not a red one. Mindful gambles are necessary for growth. Learn the art of calculated and well-timed risks and your dreams will gain staying power. As Nelson Mandela said, "It is only impossible until it's done."

The danger with stodgy Saturn in your visionary ninth house is that it can create doubt, leaving you blocked and stuck. When you feel daunted, keep learning and asking questions. Since the ninth house rules higher education, consider a return to school or seeking formal training in your field. Credentials count under Saturn's rule, and hey, it never hurts to strive toward greater mastery in your field. Strengthen any weak areas with a mentor or through formal training. Travel for business or steady work with a long-distance client is possible, or you may take concrete steps to launch an independent business. Slow and steady, which is the preferred pace for your sign, is the way.

Saturn Meets Pluto:
Life-changing adventures.

December 20, 2019-February 5, 2020

Saturn and Pluto are both in Capricorn, but they've been progressing at different paces up until now. The two luminaries will finally make contact from December 20, 2019 until February 5, 2020. Structured Saturn rules the material world, while Pluto governs the unseen. Under this Saturn-Pluto alliance, hidden truths come to light and your beliefs take on tangible form. The saying "Your thoughts create reality" will ring stunningly true now.

With serious Saturn in the philosophical ninth house, you could seek deeper wisdom through a formal spiritual practice or an organized religious community. If you're wondering, "What is this all for, anyway?" answers may start showing up. When the student is ready—and it seems this year that you are—the teacher appears.

Vision quest? Saturn and Pluto will help you gain discipline around your beliefs and faith, whatever form that might take. But if you've been content to skim the surface of spirituality, you'll be called into the depths as 2019 comes to a close. With a solar eclipse falling on December 26 in Capricorn, any lightning-bolt epiphanies could translate into a whole new life direction, one that aligns with your deepened or newfound philosophies.

Cancer/Capricorn Eclipses:
Taking the long view.

January 5, July 2 & 16, December 26

Say what? Not only will you have a flood of new ideas, Taurus, you'll become far less inhibited about discussing them. From July 2018 until July 2020, a series of change-making eclipses will fall in Cancer and Capricorn, activating your axis of communication. Four of 2019's five eclipses will be in these signs, bringing exciting new people, brainstorms and ways of seeing the world.

Eclipses pull us far beyond the familiar and help us discover new facets of ourselves—whether we were looking or not! In January, July and December, you could have some major a-ha moments that arrive unexpectedly. These eclipses will help you clarify your ideas and evolve your mindset, then give you the courage to go public with them. Over the next couple years you could become quite the media maven.

Cancer rules your third house of local events and short trips, and on July 2, a solar (new moon) eclipse here could spark a fresh start close to home, perhaps with a sibling, colleague, neighbor or friend. You may adopt a new role in your 'hood: taking a seat on city council or opening a pop-up shop. (Mayor Taurus has a ring to it…) Writing, teaching and media may be focal points now. Sign up for a short class or find a couple new local hotspots instead of going to the same-old haunts.

But don't get too comfortable at your new Michelin-starred steakhouse or community crafting café, Bull. The other three eclipses will fall in Capricorn and your worldly ninth house, which will pull you out into the wider world. Exciting travel opportunities may crop up out of the blue in January, July and December. There will be two solar (new moon) eclipses in Cap on January 5 and December 26, which could spark anything from a life-changing vacation to an indie business idea to a return to school for a degree or certification.

January's eclipse is in close proximity to stalwart Saturn, which might help formalize your big plans or bring a seasoned veteran into your orbit who helps move the action ahead quickly.

A long-distance or cross-cultural connection could ignite at the July 16 lunar (full moon) eclipse in Capricorn. Taureans who tenaciously cling to "old-school" thinking may have a huge perspective change, as this eclipse inspires you to adopt new views. Your contact with people from wildly different backgrounds or upbringings might be downright transformational, especially since this eclipse will be near shape-shifter Pluto. Having a "metaphysical moment" can be exciting, so embrace the new wisdom that floods in now. An opportunity to travel, teach or launch a visionary project could also arise this summer.

Since the ninth house rules truth-telling, this eclipse could bring a powerful moment of honesty. Being authentic can feel scary in the moment, but at least you'll know where you stand with people. Any friendships built on falsehoods will be tested. You have nothing to lose and everything to gain from keeping it real. Someone else might serve up the unvarnished truth, causing you to confront where you've buried your head in the sand.

Stay woke, Taurus—you could become a powerful "voice of the people" and an ambassador who bridges and heals divides. Commit to educating yourself first, then sharing that knowledge and insight with others.

Final Leo Eclipse:
A place to call home?

January 21

What does "home" mean to you, Taurus? On January 21, your roots get a rejuvenation as a Leo total lunar (full moon) eclipse lands in your fourth house of family, emotional foundations and all things domestic. This is the grand finale of an eclipse series that's fallen on the Leo/Aquarius axis since February 2017, transforming both your personal and professional paths. Three change-making eclipses in Aquarius landed in your ambitious tenth house, which gave your career a makeover in 2017 and 2018.

January's final Leo eclipse in your domestic fourth house may bring one more wave of changes to your living situation, a family matter or your relationship with a parent or child. You've been going back and forth on this matter for two years, and this last eclipse could finally bring the security you've been seeking—both emotionally and at home. You might also achieve the work-life balance that's eluded you for the past two years. A powerful and confident woman might play into events at this eclipse. Set your pride aside and allow her to lead the way.

Chiron in Aries:
Confronting your shadow.

February 18, 2019-April 14, 2027

Time to finally confront that issue, Taurus? A journey of deep and transformative healing begins this February, as Chiron, the comet that's now considered a minor planet, starts an extended voyage through Aries and your twelfth house of closure and compassion.

In Greek mythology, Chiron was the "wounded healer," a philosopher and teacher who could help everyone else, but couldn't fix his own issues. Chiron reveals how we can heal others through doing our own deep inner work. As the saying goes, we teach what we need to learn.

With Chiron in your twelfth house, you may confront a fear of asserting boundaries or a tendency toward escapism through vices and addictions. Taurus, you're one of the zodiac's most sensual and sensory sign, and you might tend to shield yourself from feeling pain and past trauma by eating, drinking, shopping or through some form of binge behavior. With your strong provider nature, you could also be drawn to tortured souls who end up draining you.

As Chiron pulls you out of denial and avoidance, get ready to replace cheap-fuel coping mechanisms with a sustainable source of spiritual strength. It could be meditation, using your own creativity or joining a formal faith-based community. Codependent relationships will also need to shift.

With Chiron in your esoteric twelfth house, some Bulls will discover or develop extrasensory gifts, such as clairvoyant or clairaudient abilities. In the past, your down-to-earth sign might have been quick to dismiss prophetic dreams or "signs," but now you'll find too much evidence to just overlook them. You might be drawn to explore topics such as the Law of Attraction and the quantum realm, or even do some shamanic healing.

Chiron was already briefly in Aries from April 17 to September 25, 2018 and in 2019, it will settle into Aries for a longer trip, staying until April 14, 2027. Over the next eight years, prepare to move beyond what your five senses reveal and take an unexpected caravan trip through the mystical and metaphysical. You could emerge with your own Taurus-approved version of practical magic that bridges the material and spiritual and helps others transform in a safe, grounded way. ✳

MONTHLY HOTSPOTS

JANUARY: LOVE HOTSPOTS

January 7-February 3: Venus in Sagittarius

As amorous Venus makes her annual tour of your seductive eighth house, you'll get the year off to a smoldering start. A relationship could advance to the next stage of commitment, and for single Bulls, the chemistry will be off the charts.

January 18: Venus-Mars trine

This rare and heartwarming mashup of the love planets in your most sensitive houses encourages you to drop your guard and be open to receiving support and affection. Whether you're with your longstanding partner or a promising love interest, this day could be one of the most magical of the year.

January 20: Venus-Neptune square

Everyone's got an opinion but listen *very* selectively. Neptune is sensitive and heightens intuition, but when it squares emotional Venus, it can distort facts and make you confused, jealous and even paranoid. Take a timeout from your dating apps and meet friends for some lighthearted IRL fun instead.

January 21: Leo full moon (total lunar eclipse and supermoon)

Today's powerful eclipse—the "grand finale" in a series on the Leo/Aquarius axis that began in February 2017—may affect you on a profoundly deep level. Strong emotions can rise to the surface when this lunation lands in your sensitive fourth house. Looking to make changes on the home front? Get the ball rolling now, and over the next six months, you could be in your new digs, with a different roommate (or your partner), and perhaps a new addition to the family! Relations with your mother, a child or a female relative may be pivotal today. Look back to what happened in your life following the February 10, 2017, and January 31, 2018, eclipses for clues.

January 22: Venus-Jupiter meetup

Feeling adventurous? This once-a-year sync-up of the zodiac's "benefics" in your intense, erotic eighth house could open the door to some frisky exploration with an intimate connection. You could also take a leap of faith and get vulnerable, opening up emotionally.

January 25: Mars-Jupiter trine

You'll be eager to jump into a personal or business relationship under today's mashup of these two celestial go-getters. While you're confident that it will work out brilliantly, do the requisite checks before you commit. This rare mashup prompts you to take calculated risks—just make sure they really are smart ones.

JANUARY: CAREER HOTSPOTS

January 2: Sun-Saturn meetup

Under this once-a-year mashup of the ego-driven Sun and tempered Saturn in your visionary zone, you could receive priceless advice from an entrepreneurial mentor or industry pioneer. It's a great day to test the practicality of a business idea. If it does stand the test of time, you could earn a rep as a trailblazer in your industry.

January 4: Mercury-Uranus trine

Don't stick to common sense or the same-old thinking under this revolutionary meetup. Tap your intuition and, if you're still stuck, turn to the work hivemind to help you unravel a vexing problem. Try free-writing or taking a walk to hit your own mental refresh button.

January 4-24: Mercury in Capricorn

Has the inspiration well run dry? Refill it by stimulating your imagination in unexpected ways. Over the next couple weeks, make a special effort to stretch beyond your comfort zone. Take a walk in a totally unfamiliar part of town—perhaps one packed with art galleries, live music and crafts. Wander into bookstores and funky boutiques. Limit conversation to positive, high-minded subjects, and when you come back to any stymied projects, you're sure to see them *very* differently.

January 5: Capricorn new moon (partial solar eclipse)

The first of 2019's two Capricorn new moons can help you get a dream project off the ground. This galvanizing eclipse falls near structured Saturn, so things could come together quickly and form a rock-solid foundation. The caveat: You may have to take a risk to pull this off. Do you believe in your heart this is worth doing? If so, write out your plan, then take that first giant leap of faith!

January 6: Uranus retrograde ends

Changemaker Uranus resumes forward motion after five unsteady months, part of which were spent reversing through your healing and transitional twelfth house. What's left to release, forgive or transmute into gold? This is the side-spinning planet's last hurrah in Aries for another 84 years before he puts down roots in Taurus on March 6, sticking around in your sign until April 2026. Rip that bandage off and release those self-defeating habits and relationships over the next two months.

January 8: Mercury-Mars square

Roll up your psychic sleeves and take a hard look at some unsavory behavior in your inner circle (including your own). This edgy clash can ratchet up bickering, backstabbing and rivalry. Don't let the red planet fool you into believing that aggressive or pushy behavior is ever permissible.

January 11: Sun-Pluto meetup

Keep your eye fixed on the prize today, Bull. This once-a-year, game-changing merger of the potent Sun and calculating Pluto helps you see beyond the obvious and take a long-sighted glimpse at what's possible. A powerful person may be intrigued by your ideas, but if they're proprietary, ask them to sign a nondisclosure agreement first. (True pros seldom balk at that request.) Play your cards right and this could open doors to a prestigious opportunity.

January 13: Mercury-Saturn meetup

Think before you speak today! With grounded Saturn bolstering the communication planet, your verbal skills will not fail you. Don't get tripped up over the details, though. All you really need to do is clearly explain the big picture and what exactly you propose to do, along with what resources you need to pull it off. Play up what's in it for them, and you'll have no problem gaining their support.

January 13: Jupiter-Neptune square

Bigger isn't always better, and faster doesn't always get you to the finish line first (or more contentedly). This clash between these two starry-eyed planets could cause you to be a little off the mark, even gullible. If you're going to jump out of a metaphorical plane, make sure in advance that the parachute works!

January 18: Mercury-Pluto meetup

You're in the zone, and your mind is racing 100 miles ahead of everyone else's in the room. Be patient, and let people catch up to you. When they do, hit 'em with your sharpest elevator pitch and land this deal!

January 18: Sun-Uranus square

You might get an inexplicable urge to blurt out something that inadvertently offends someone.

It'll be hard to keep your opinions to yourself, so if you must express them, make sure you have an appropriate audience. Closed-minded people—or strangers who don't know you and aren't familiar with your dry humor—could take your words out of context and use them against you.

January 21: Leo full moon (total lunar eclipse and supermoon)

This eclipse is the cherry on top of a two-year series on the Leo/Aquarius axis that began in February 2017. Things in your home and work lives may have shifted in dramatic ways since then, and today could bring a culmination point. Need a hint? Reflect back to the events that followed the earlier eclipses on February 10, 2017, and January 31, 2018.

January 23: Mercury-Uranus square

Expressive Mercury is at odds with disruptor Uranus in your indirect twelfth house. Your words may not reflect your true feelings, or at the last minute you might throw someone a curveball. If you need to get something off your chest, *try to* find a diplomatic way to do so.

January 24-February 10: Mercury in Aquarius

Speak up, Taurus! There's no good reason to keep your innovative ideas to yourself. Over the next three weeks, articulate Mercury will cruise through your tenth house of career and ambition, helping you analyze a big move you want to make or propose. Take adequate time to research and polish your strategic plan before delivering your presentation to the decision-makers.

       The AstroTwins' 2019 Planetary Planner

January 25: Mars-Jupiter trine

Trust your gut and put it all out there. Under this expansive pairing of assertive Mars and enthusiastic Jupiter, you're supported in going big and bold. Need help? Turning to the right person can cut your workload in half.

FEBRUARY: LOVE HOTSPOTS

February 2: Venus-Uranus trine

Careful where you turn your gaze. Out of the blue, a dazzling connection or attraction could blaze up. Single? Your seductive powers could be like catnip to the right person, so wield them selectively. Attached? Drop the steel gates and get even closer on a deep emotional level. Caution: Since Uranus can dredge things up from deeply buried places, strong emotions can explode without warning.

February 3-March 1: Venus in Capricorn

The love planet begins her annual strut through your adventurous and global ninth house. You might widen your search parameters on dating apps (and don't completely rule out long-distance suitors, as long as it's temporary) or simply take a whole new approach to amorous and intimate relations. For couples, it's a great time for a romantic getaway.

February 13: Mars-Uranus meetup

Red-blooded Mars and erratic Uranus form their biennial union, conspiring in your clandestine twelfth house. Think you're holding it together emotionally? Watch what happens when *that* person presses your buttons. Do your utmost to restrain yourself, whether that means writing your angry response in your journal rather than sending an email or *not* confessing your undying love in a late-night tipsy text.

February 14-March 31: Mars in Taurus

Hello, hotness! The lusty love god sprints through your sign for six weeks, making you feel frisky, sexy and adventurous. You can't help but turn heads wherever you go, so be prepared to attract a lot of attention. It's up to you, of course, what (if anything) you choose to do about that.

February 18: Venus-Saturn meetup

Having fun is lovely, but under this once-a-year union of romantic Venus and serious Saturn, your focus turns to the future. What do you want for the romantic long-term? Venus can do fantasy with the best of 'em, but grounded Saturn would rather have a candid convo about your goals and dreams.

February 19: Virgo full supermoon

Make the most of this sensual, steamy lunation in your fifth house of amour and glamour, amplified by its supermoon status. Your desires will be palpable, and if you're unattached, this is a prime opportunity to flex your flirting muscles. Attached? Do something that smacks of old-fashioned romance. Watch for drama, as strong emotions could surge up under this expressive moon.

February 22: Venus-Pluto meetup

Don't settle for anything (or anyone) that doesn't float your boat. When transformational Pluto makes its annual merger with amorous Venus, you'll be inspired to raise the bar on your relationship expectations. Be clear about what you want—and what you aren't willing to put up with.

50

FEBRUARY: CAREER HOTSPOTS

February 1: Mars-Pluto square

The red planet is firing up your compassion zone, and as he clashes with manipulative Pluto, you might find the courage to stand up to an overly authoritative person. While it's admirable to advocate for fair play, you don't want to stoop to their level. Check in with your gut and find a higher-vibrational approach to neutralize them.

February 4: Aquarius new moon (Chinese New Year)

Career goals: check! This annual new moon powers up your professional zone and helps you peer into the future to map out a grand plan. Work backward: Where do you want to be by the corresponding full moon on August 15? Change starts with vision— *your* vision—and if you get clear about that now, rich opportunities could present themselves over the next six months. This is an auspicious day to send out resumes or follow up with promising leads. Today also kicks off the Chinese Year of the Earth Pig, an invitation to add a lively and personable touch to everything you do.

February 10-April 17: Mercury in Pisces

Mercury swings into your eleventh house of teamwork and technology for an extra-long stay because it will be retrograde from March 5 to 28. Don't get too frustrated if initiatives you begin this month stall or even seem to evaporate. The solid ones *will* resurface or pick up speed at the end of March.

February 14-March 31: Mars in Taurus

You've been waiting two years for this, and hopefully you're ready to hit go! Action planet Mars blasts into your sign, giving you the guts to assert yourself and fearlessly promote your work and ideas. Check in with yourself periodically to make sure you're not coming on *too* strong.

February 19: Virgo full supermoon

This culminating lunation can help you put the finishing touches on a personal project or find an inspirational new creative outlet. It also bodes well for anyone looking to fall in love, deepen a bond or start a family.

February 19: Mercury-Neptune meetup

Close the opinion polls before you lose your own point of view. While it can be valuable to turn to the hivemind when you feel stuck, too much input will confuse more than clarify a situation today. Be an active listener, but when it's your turn to speak up, make sure your voice is heard loud and clear.

February 22: Mercury-Jupiter square

Oversharer alert! Stay on-guard for TMI, as this clash can loosen lips *and* sink battleships. You might also have placed misbegotten confidence in a person or a plan that warrants more research. It's okay to let people know you're not 100 percent ready for the big reveal. They'll respect you for taking the time to get it right—and for being confident enough to admit that.

MARCH: LOVE HOTSPOTS

March 1: Venus-Uranus square

Compromise could be challenging as unpredictable Uranus sends a disruptive beam to cosmic harmonizer Venus. Fight the urge to be stubborn and inflexible. The key here is to listen and try to find a way to meet in the middle. Sometimes people simply need to feel heard.

March 1-26: Venus in Aquarius

Love and work collide in the sweetest possible way as charismatic Venus sails through your professional zone for the next three weeks. Looking for romance? Networking events can double as "singles mixers," so dress to impress. Of course, if your office has a strict no-dating policy, don't cross that line. In a long-term relationship? Get out on the scene more together and act like the power couple that you are!

March 20: Mars-Pluto trine

There's no holding back now! Whatever you've been keeping to yourself lately comes gushing out like somebody opened the floodgates. While it may feel tense or awkward at first, this declaration or confession will clear the air *and* deepen your connection. If this person can't handle your truth, take it as a red flag and reconsider the durability of the relationship.

March 21: Venus-Mars square

The passion you're feeling for someone might not be easily contained—so why bother? If this is something you simply "need" to explore, nobody's going to talk you out of it. While the heat is undeniable, be forewarned that under this uneasy clash, things might not flow as smoothly as you'd hoped.

March 26-April 20: Venus in Pisces

Today's arrival of kind-hearted Venus into Pisces and your communal eleventh house serves up your annual reminder that not everything has to have a sexual subtext. Some relationships are meant to be purely platonic, so ease off the erotic throttle and appreciate the freedom that comes from engaging without an "agenda." Single? Enjoy the opportunity to sample from the whole buffet table. Couples can reconnect with your separate circles or host a gathering together.

March 31-May 15: Mars in Gemini

As the fiery red planet enters your security-seeking second house, you get heated about locking down a steady guarantee. Be firm about what you will and won't settle for, but be careful not to come across as a dictator. This sizzling sensual cycle also whets your appetite for pleasure—just watch the price tag your luxe-loving impulses may ring up. Money can buy a lot of good times, but it can't buy true happiness.

MARCH: CAREER HOTSPOTS

March 5-28: Mercury retrograde in Pisces

Just when you thought you were getting an exciting initiative off the ground, the messenger planet goes and turns retrograde. You know the drill: Hurry up and wait! The next three weeks are likely to be chockful of delays, miscommunications and technological glitches. Since you can't micromanage things outside your control, use this time to review your work, research more deeply and reconnect to people who've fallen by the wayside.

March 6: Pisces new moon

This once-a-year reboot in your eleventh house of teamwork and technology can get the creative juices flowing! You know exactly what you want to launch into, but you may be feeling overwhelmed or unsure where to begin. You don't have to go it alone. Team up with a kindred spirit or hire a business coach to help you get the ball rolling.

March 6, 2019-April 26, 2026: Uranus in Taurus

Will the authentic and unapologetic Bulls please stand up? Revolutionary Uranus takes up long-term residence in your sign for the first time since 1942, putting down roots until 2026. You had a sneak preview of this Uranus transit last year (from May 15 to November 6), but this time, it's here to stay. While it's hard to say precisely where and how (and with whom) these radical shifts will occur, one thing's for sure: Over the next seven years, life is going to look and feel very different. Prepare to take more of a leadership role in your personal and professional realms and to pursue more freedom in general.

March 6: Sun-Neptune meetup

On super-rare days like this, when logic meets intuition, you can't help but manifest what's in your heart. Have the confidence that you can create what you want and call in what you need! Should you have a moment of doubt, turn to colleagues and close friends to reboot your mojo.

March 13: Sun-Jupiter square

Some outsized egos grandstand up a storm today, when a clash between these two confident players veers into cocky and know-it-all territory. Jealousy could stir up competition in a group. Make sure everyone feels important, rather than just one or two loud voices dominating the conversation.

March 14: Mars-Saturn trine

You've got what it takes, Taurus: Now give yourself a pep talk and negotiate for more than you were planning to ask for! With ambitious Mars synced up with structured Saturn, you have a plan and the motivation to relentlessly pursue it. Keep your door open: You may be tapped for a promotion or an enviable leadership role.

March 15: Mercury-Jupiter square

Don't promise anyone the moon today, no matter how hard they push. It'll be easy to overestimate your abilities, but that's a dangerous proposition. Stay humble and, if anything, lowball your deliverables. If you're the one taking pitches, don't believe half of what people are telling you!

March 20: Libra full supermoon

This empowering lunation gives you the vision and the drive to tackle a major project that will ultimately make your work life more streamlined and efficient. But first you've got to level a mountain of papers and miscellany that's slowing your roll. Lucky for you, this year serves up a rare double header of Libra full moons in your organized sixth house (the next is a month from now). Today, come up with a master plan, and slowly but surely plow through it over the coming four weeks.

March 24: Mercury-Neptune meetup

Brilliant ideas can come out of collaborative brainstorming sessions, but don't get so carried away by the enthusiastic energy in the room that you're blinded to obvious holes in the logic. Listen and be present in the moment, but take good notes and later, on your own, make sure they're actually doable.

March 28: Mercury retrograde ends

Team tension dissipates at last! As Mercury ends its dicey three-week retrograde in your group and technology zone, it's safe to resume a collaboration and ramp up your social media presence.

       The AstroTwins' 2019 Planetary Planner

March 31-May 15: Mars in Gemini

When the action planet returns to your second house of work and money for the first time in two years, you'll be more than ready to leap into a project or a deal that holds promise for a big payday. Keep an eye on this so it doesn't balloon out of control. Have a plan to blow off steam since Mars can rev up the stress and pressure as much as the excitement.

APRIL: LOVE HOTSPOTS

April 5: Aries new moon

The year's only Aries new moon churns up some intense emotions in your house of healing, release and transitions. It's not easy for your steadfast sign to let things (and especially people) go, but this is your once-a-year golden opportunity to move on from something that's been holding you back. Dial up the compassion and gratitude—and step into your exciting new chapter!

April 10: Venus-Neptune meetup

You'll have stars in your eyes and a spring in your step under today's dreamy alignment of love-planet Venus and fantasy-spinner Neptune in your friendship corner. Keeping it platonic will take extreme discipline, but look ahead: Are you willing to mess up a solid connection for a night (or week) of pleasure? Or might this be the real thing?

April 10-August 11: Jupiter retrograde in Sagittarius

This annual reversal of expansive Jupiter, this year through your eighth house of intense emotions and sexuality, gives you a rare opportunity to sort through some deep feelings. Reflect on your connection to someone else but also yourself and how you "do" intimate relations. Don't rush to the finish line on this one. Take a time out to process your emotions and get a handle on how you really feel here.

April 15: Venus-Jupiter square

It might seem like you're being yanked in diverging directions as thirsty Jupiter clashes with amorous Venus, making you itch for freedom or a new conquest. Since this is a fast-moving, one-day transit, hold off doing anything drastic.

April 20-May 15: Venus in Aries

The love planet commences her annual parade through intrepid Aries—and for you, this activates your internally focused twelfth house. Your thoughts will churn with dreamy fantasies, but it might take a few weeks (until she enters Taurus) to actually do anything about them. Careful not to assign idealized qualities to someone who can't actually live up to them.

APRIL: CAREER HOTSPOTS

April 10: Sun-Saturn square

Ignore that little voice inside you that's trying to undermine your confidence. This is an old script—and it no longer has relevance in your life. Stay alert for a person who's trying to provoke or unnerve you. Don't engage—that's what they want. Instead, ignore them and pour twice as much effort into your own work. Success truly is the best revenge!

April 10-August 11: Jupiter retrograde in Sagittarius

Even when it's retrograde, Jupiter can bring growth and luck, but when it does take its annual backspin—this year through your house of long-range financial goals and shared resources—the message is to slow down with all investments and joint ventures. Taking time to review and reflect is always a good idea. If there's debt to be paid off, chip away at it more aggressively now.

April 12: Mercury-Jupiter square
Today's stars come with a TMI alert. There really is such a thing as excessive input, especially when it's inconsistent and you don't know who to believe—if anyone. Take it all with a grain of salt, and when you reach your saturation point, let people know you're going to sleep on it, which is exactly what you should do.

April 13: Sun-Pluto square
Things may not be—make that *won't be*—as they seem today under this shadowy clash. With master manipulator Pluto running interference on the truth, it will be hard to tell whether someone's all talk or can actually back up their words with action. Best bet: Listen to their pitch, then ask for solid proof of their claims.

April 17-May 6: Mercury in Aries
These next three weeks offer you a lot of practice balancing your brain's analytical left hemisphere with the more intuitive and creative right. The mental planet is out of its element in your internally focused twelfth house, so rather than embark on a big new project, wrap up anything that's not quite nailed down. Spinning your wheels in analysis paralysis? Let yourself dream, journal, meditate and vision-board your way to an answer (yes, really!).

April 19: Libra full moon
The second of two Libra full moons in a row (the first was on March 20) lights up your efficient sixth house. Put systems in place, hire and fire, do a major spring decluttering. A detailed project you started last month could move past the finish line. Lean in and get 'er done!

April 22: Sun-Uranus meetup
This once-a-year alignment is a strongly-worded invitation to take a gamble on something you know in your heart is worth the risk. How to tell if it's really the right thing? If it's sure to disrupt the status quo—in a positive way—that's your winner.

April 24-October 3: Pluto retrograde in Capricorn
Just when you were convinced your grand idea was "too big to fail," transformational Pluto switches direction, causing you to doubt yourself. Don't worry if the visions get a little hazy. This is your cue to go back and make sure it's exactly what you want—and 100 percent doable.

April 27: Mars-Neptune square
Reality check! You're eager to get a job finished, but success will feel hollow if you have to take any seedy shortcuts or step on any toes to get there. Watch for someone promising way more than seems doable. Neptune can dial up intuition and confusion, so take the "better safe than sorry" route.

April 29-September 18: Saturn retrograde in Capricorn
When the planet of time and structure makes his annual backflip—this year in your visionary ninth

house—you may realize that you need to scale back or roll something out in phases. Think "slow and steady" rather than trying to speed your ideas into production. It'll be worth it in the long run.

MAY: LOVE HOTSPOTS

May 7: Venus-Saturn square
A little fantasy goes a long way, but you don't want to get carried away with improbable daydreams. With the amorous planet in your dreamy twelfth house, you may have stars in your eyes. But today's reality-checking square from solemn Saturn rips off those rose-colored aviators and forces you to deal with the human being who's right in front of you, warts and all.

May 9: Venus-Jupiter trine
This rare heart-opening beam encourages you to take a risk in the name of amour and share from the deepest level of your being, even if—*especially if*—it makes you feel vulnerable.

May 9: Venus-Pluto square
You may be forced to see someone for who they truly are, not who you want them to be. If you've put them up on a pedestal, cut through the illusions. When it comes to dating, keep your skepticism intact and make people earn your awe!

May 15-June 8: Venus in Taurus
It's a magical few weeks when your planetary protector, charming Venus, swirls through your sign. You'll feel beautiful and flirty again, and as a result, you'll be magnetically attractive. Single? Have your fun, but don't settle!

May 15-July 1: Mars in Cancer
When unabashed Mars blasts into your communication sector, you'll be bold and assertive, unafraid to make the first move with someone you've been interested in. Couples: This is a good time to broach a difficult subject, but watch that you don't come on too aggressively.

May 18: Venus-Uranus meetup
It's hard to prepare for curveballs, but knowing they're coming can at least keep you on your guard. Under this unpredictable pairing, sudden sparks could fly—or there might be an out-of-the-blue shakeup.

May 18: Scorpio full moon
This could be a "make it or break" day, when you finally decide whether to go all in or cut bait. Scorpio doesn't play by half measures, and under the year's only full moon in your partnership house, you'll be strong and clear in your resolution. Single? This heady lunar lift could light a path to a prospect with soulmate potential.

May 31: Venus-Saturn trine
Under this twice-a-year alignment of the love planet and future-focused Saturn, you may tire of head games and "the chase" and call someone on their waffling. You're all about commitment, so stop talking and take the plunge. If you're the one who's been on the fence, consult the Magic Eight Ball and do *something*!

MAY: CAREER HOTSPOTS

May 1: Mercury-Saturn square
This reprised transit from March 11 can help you

(finally) set some clear boundaries and manage people's expectations—starting with your own. Feeling overwhelmed by a project that's ballooned out of control? Pull the emergency brake. Map things out in manageable chunks, and then take one methodical step at a time.

May 2: Mercury-Pluto square

Someone may not be the supportive ally they claim to be, so proceed cautiously. If you discover that a colleague isn't being upfront, don't call them on it just yet. Under this slippery square, they'll wriggle out of accountability or possibly even start a resentful vendetta against you. Just maintain your distance and do your own thing for now. But do keep a paper trail (and a handy witness) if anything shady seems afoot.

May 2: Mercury-Jupiter trine

Trust your gut more than spreadsheets today. This rare cosmic mashup of analysis and intuition sharpens your thoughts and heightens your inner knowing. Gather some creative minds together for a brainstorming jam. You might hit on the next big thing.

May 4: Taurus new moon

The year's only new moon in your sign is a huge deal, bringing the potential to start an exciting new chapter in your life. What do you need to release in order to make a new beginning? When that door closes, another will blow wide open. Set some intentions for the rest of the year, then horns down and charge ahead!

May 5: Mars-Jupiter opposition

Being a risk-taker is great, but not if it leads you to gamble away your hard-earned capital. If you're considering a financial move that's borderline foolish, stop and run it past a few fiscally savvy friends—and maybe a professional adviser. Get some tips on differentiating between a smart investment and a Ponzi scheme.

May 6-21: Mercury in Taurus

The communication planet is taking its annual lap through your sign, pulling you up on the pulpit and handing you the mic. What message do you want to put out to the masses? What big ask do you need to make? You've got the next couple weeks to make some bold and assertive moves.

May 8: Mercury-Uranus meetup

This is the first of a handful of such alignments over the coming seven years. Your mind will be racing with innovative ideas, and with Mercury and Uranus both in your grounded sign, you'll have the patience and foresight to plan well and see the right ventures through to completion. This is how you turn a dream into a reality.

May 11: Sun-Saturn trine

Trust issues could flare with a potential collaborator. You don't have to give them a polygraph exam; just test the waters with a low-risk joint project. Their performance will quickly let you know whether there's solid potential here or not.

May 13: Sun-Pluto trine

Go big! You're sitting on an idea that could blow up if it's developed properly. Take one significant step today to see how viable it really is. This may be the moment when people realize what a creative visionary you truly are!

 The AstroTwins' 2019 Planetary Planner

May 15-July 1: Mars in Cancer

Motivated Mars zooms into your communication house today, cranking up the social engagements and action on the local scene for the next six weeks. Don't just sit there *thinking* about things you want to do. Get up and get moving!

May 16: Mercury-Saturn trine

Ideas are a dime a dozen, but when you can put a firm timeline and structure to them, they're far more likely to succeed. Under this solidifying alignment, get your thoughts on paper and share them with a well-connected person, someone who might be interested in funding it or maybe even partnering up.

May 18: Scorpio full moon

Still laboring on your own? Drop your burden and find a like-minded partner! This major annual event in your house of committed relationships could shine a light on the perfect collaborator. Just note: You'll have to be willing to compromise—not a Taurean strong suit.

May 18: Mercury-Pluto trine

Get thee to the negotiating table! There's a hot deal you're eager to close, so bring the parties together today. Your analytical abilities will be laser-sharp, and you'll clearly see how all the pieces can best be used to everyone's benefit.

May 21-June 4: Mercury in Gemini

This annual transit puts financial matters front and center. Don't just "wing it" or let your funds languish in a no-interest account. Do some research, talk to an adviser, and make your money work as hard for you as you do for it.

May 29: Mercury-Neptune square

Pause before you poll your friends and feeds for opinions! With Mercury in your practical second house, you don't need all the extra noise that befuddling Neptune in your groups sector will bring. Instead of putting static on your own line, trust that you know what's best—or at least, only ask a few selectively-curated (and experienced!) people for their input.

May 30: Mercury-Jupiter opposition

You may be eager to sign a contract or jump into a partnership with someone who seems highly promising, but stop and play out a few different scenarios in your head, including "worst-case." You need solid proof that this person can deliver what they're dangling before you put your own time or money on the line.

JUNE: LOVE HOTSPOTS

June 2: Venus-Pluto trine

Why keep your desires to yourself? The best way to get them fulfilled is to let people know what you're feeling. Today, as alchemical Pluto sends a supportive beam to the love planet, share what's in your heart—and watch what happens when you do!

June 8-July 3: Venus in Gemini

This annual transit can motivate you to upgrade those aspects of your lifestyle where you've been cutting corners. Over these next three weeks, do something that makes you feel more stable and pampered. With beautifying Venus in this chic zone, bring more style and sophistication to your world. Dress up and put extra effort into the way you present yourself. Single? You could meet someone through work or at an "upscale" social spot. For couples, this is a great transit for splurging on a few decadent dates to remember.

June 16: Jupiter-Neptune square
It's great to be hopeful, but you don't want to cross the line into being unrealistic or even gullible. If you're in a relationship, don't make assumptions—come out and ask about anything that isn't crystal-clear. Single? Run the necessary background checks before you get in too deep with someone new.

June 17: Sagittarius full moon
The year's only Sagittarius full moon powers up your erotic, seductive eighth house. Ready to take your next step in the commitment department? This lunar light can illuminate the perfect path for getting there. The next two weeks are ideal for deep bonding and emotional sharing, even if that means getting a little vulnerable.

June 23: Venus-Jupiter opposition
Need a romantic reboot? There are plenty of ways to spice things up that won't push you out of your comfort zone or damage each other's trust. One thing *not* to do is look for cheap thrills outside the relationship—unless you're willing to risk what you've got. Single? Don't take people at their word. Today's stars can cause them to exaggerate or totally misrepresent who they really are.

June 24: Venus-Neptune square
Confused about a love issue? Don't go running to your inner circle for answers. Tune in to your own higher wisdom. The more you do this, the stronger the guidance will become. Remember: This is about *you*, not them!

June 26-July 19: Mercury in Leo
With the communication planet sailing through your private fourth house for the first of two visits this year, you'll have a chance to slow down, get quiet and process some heavy emotions. This is a time where it's actually helpful to delve into sensitive topics and even get a little teary-eyed or nostalgic. Ditch that practical, gruff exterior and let your sentimental side out.

JUNE: CAREER HOTSPOTS

June 3: Gemini new moon
When the year's only Gemini new moon activates your second house of security and finances, you could finally be ready to take a bold step toward changing your job or nailing down a side business. In social Gemini, la luna nudges you to reach out to people who might help you get a toe in the right door.

June 4-26: Mercury in Cancer
With curious and social Mercury beaming through your communication corner, the brainstorms come fast and furious. Get some power lunches on the books and schedule a few ideas-generating meetings. To the degree possible, clear out your schedule so you can dedicate yourself to a writing, media or video project. This is the first of Mercury's two trips through Cancer in 2019 thanks to a retrograde next month, during which the messenger planet will park here from July 19 to August 11.

June 9: Sun-Neptune square
If there's one thing your reliable sign can't tolerate, it's erratic or flaky colleagues. You've been working too hard to see your project unravel, so before this happens, run interference. To ensure you meet your

The AstroTwins' 2019 Planetary Planner

own deadline, keep those social media websites closed!

June 10: Sun-Jupiter opposition

It's easy to get a bit over-confident under this one-day mashup, but don't trust important things to other people or luck. Certain projections or calculations may be off the mark, so before you talk to the power brokers, triple-check all your numbers!

June 14: Mars-Neptune trine

Your powers of persuasion are exceptionally high today, and if you're selling something, people may line up to get in on the deal. Keep your sales pitch understated, and take the time to answer everyone's questions. Focus on how this product or service can make their life better or easier. Are you the decision-maker? Heartstrings can be easily tugged now, so guard against guilt trips or saying "yes" just because you like someone.

June 14: Mars-Saturn opposition

Although you've got charisma in spades from today's Mars-Neptune meetup, don't promise more than you can deliver. Boundary-hound Saturn throws down a stern reminder not to rush. If you're not sure something is ready for the big reveal, let people know it's "close" but that you need more time to tweak a few last things. Before taking it public, do a soft launch so you don't waste any time and money.

June 16: Mercury-Neptune trine

You can read other people like large-print books today, as this perceptive pairing sharpens both your logical and intuitive powers. And since Mercury and Neptune will ping each other from your interpersonal houses, it's a perfect day for meetings, pitches, interviews and finesse-ing your most important work relationships. Networking events can turn up surprising serendipities.

June 16: Mercury-Saturn opposition

You're eager to get a big idea out to the world, but you don't want to do so prematurely. A beam from cautious Saturn can help you slow down and do the necessary beta-testing to get it right before you launch.

June 16: Jupiter-Neptune square

Don't put the cart before the horse. Today's expansive starmap could make you a bit unrealistic or impractical. There's a time and place for big-picture thinking and a time to narrow the focus and nail down the minutiae. Today calls for the latter.

June 17: Sagittarius full moon

This once-a-year lunation powers up your eighth house of long-term wealth, investments and shared resources. Things you've been working on and building toward for the past six months could finally reach an important tipping point. Celebrate the victory, but start working on the next phase to ensure the highest level of success.

June 18: Mercury-Mars meetup

Talks could get heated—or at least intense—as passionate Mars and chatty Mercury unite in your expressive third house. Your mind is racing and you're hyped up to take action on a new idea. If you feel clear about next steps, then don't hesitate. Strike while the iron is hot.

June 19: Mercury-Pluto opposition

Yesterday you felt clear as a bell, and today seems strewn with hidden agendas and cryptic mixed messages. Read between the lines and assume nothing, as upfront Mercury and secretive Pluto are at cross-purposes. Beware a charming person's masterful manipulations.

June 19: Mars-Pluto opposition

Hold your fire! Today, as aggro Mars clashes with alchemical Pluto in your candid communication corners, things could get said that both of you regret. Resist the temptation to hit below the belt, and keep it professional. If you realize you need a neutral party to resolve the conflict, don't hesitate to find one!

June 21-November 27: Neptune retrograde in Pisces

Back away from the "difficult people." As draining Neptune turns retrograde in your collaborative eleventh house, you could get sucked into dramas with energy vampires and trolls, both in person and online. Resist the temptation to mediate warring factions at work and stay focused on your own mission. If you're having second thoughts about working with someone, put the project on hold for the summer.

JULY: LOVE HOTSPOTS

July 1-August 18: Mars in Leo

For the first time in two years, intensifier Mars marches into your fourth house of home and family. On the upside, this could give you the motivation you need to make a change, whether a redecorating project or a move. But since the red planet can stir up strong emotions, this may lead to some conflicts on the home front or someone acting out their anger or jealousy. Knowing this energy is in the air might help you be a little more patient with a loved one who's hurting. But that doesn't mean you have to be their emotional punching bag!

July 3-27: Venus in Cancer

This short-but-sweet transit of gentle Venus through your third house of socializing and local happenings can bring some levity to your romantic life. Single? You may discover a whole new side to a platonic pal or have a serendipitous chat with someone you meet hanging in your 'hood. Attached? Mix it up by getting out and taking in more live performances.

July 17: Venus-Saturn opposition

Tempers could flare under this critical clash, so make sure you're not the one dealing out the harsh words. Since "discussions" can quickly turn into heated arguments if you're not mindful, stay on-guard to avoid getting sucked into one.

July 18: Venus-Neptune trine

What's your hottest aphrodisiac under this dream-weaving mashup? Nope, not strawberries and champagne, but stimulating (and seductive) conversation. Enjoy the ride but know that this person may not be "the one"—and it doesn't matter. Practice the art of being in the moment and simply enjoy connecting with a kindred soul.

July 21: Venus-Pluto opposition

Your emotions may be all over the map today as the amorous planet butts heads with intensifier Pluto. Some part of you is eager to connect on a deeper level, yet childhood issues or fear may be blocking you from "going there." If this is a fairly

The AstroTwins' 2019 Planetary Planner

solid relationship, open up to your partner and let them know what you're going through so they don't misinterpret your behavior.

July 24: Mercury-Venus meetup

When the cosmic messenger teams up with the love planet in your communication house, you'll have the gift of gab *and* the compassion to broach a tricky subject—or let someone how you really feel about them.

July 27-August 21: Venus in Leo

If your mojo's been in slow-mo, this annual romantic reboot can give you a jumpstart. When vixen Venus grooves into passionate Leo and your domestic zone, you may not have to leave the house to find romance. But you might have to take your dating apps a bit more seriously and line up a few low-key dates. Family members may fix you up or, for couples, talk could turn to meeting each other's relatives, exchanging keys or moving in together.

July 31: Leo new moon

This once-a-year lunar lift in your fourth house of domesticity and emotional foundations is a perfect time to launch a new chapter around home, family or lifestyle. You might suddenly decide to buy or sell real estate or to expand your family. Just make sure you're acting out of desire, not any external pressure.

JULY: CAREER HOTSPOTS

July 1-August 18: Mars in Leo

With this cosmic energy boost in your domestic fourth house, you might reorganize your workspace—or launch a home-based business. Mars can ratchet up tension, so try to stay in control of your emotions and don't let tension from your personal life derail your professional goals.

July 2: Cancer new moon (solar eclipse)

At this rare eclipse in your expressive third house, devote yourself to enhancing your communication skills. Deliberately listen more in conversations, instead of interrupting or anxiously formulating your response before they even finish. With coworkers, let them express their ideas without your feeling the need to edit or judge. Once innovative ideas are on the table, you can always fine-tune them in the months to come.

July 7-31: Mercury retrograde

Back up your data, try not to sign contracts, and put everything in writing—in clear, concise language—while the messenger planet backspins through your privacy-seeking fourth house. Things could get really slippery for the last few days, when Mercury dips back into your communication zone on July 19. But if you don't take anything for granted, you can minimize the "damage."

July 8: Mercury-Mars meetup

Mental Mercury and motivator Mars meet up again, this time while Mercury is retrograde. If there's an old idea that still has potential, consider putting a little elbow grease into it. You never know: It might have legs once you revive it with some TLC!

July 9: Sun-Saturn opposition

Cautious Saturn flashes a warning light your way, insisting you protect your personal boundaries and not cross *any* lines in the sand! If you've promised more than you can realistically deliver, come right out and ask for more time or a little assistance.

July 10: Sun-Neptune trine

Start your day with the intention to give others the floor and be more of an objective supporter. You've got some big ideas of your own, but you also know how powerful the right collaborators can be. Before you attempt to bring them on-board *your* project, let them see what a genuinely fair-minded team player you are.

July 11: Mars-Uranus square

While it's hard to predict exactly what this wild and wooly starmap will unleash, it's probably safe to say that today won't be a mellow and uneventful day. Someone's ego could get out of hand, and in general, emotions will be running high. The best thing you can do with these hot-headed planets going mano-a-mano is keep a low profile and watch your own fiery temper.

July 14: Sun-Pluto opposition

Words can be like daggers today, as manipulative Pluto faces off with the ego-driven Sun across your communication axis. Power struggles could erupt, and a less-than-honorable person might try to advance their own self-interested agenda.

July 16: Capricorn full moon (lunar eclipse)

This once-a-year event powers up your expansive ninth house, and because it lands alongside alchemical Pluto, you might finally achieve liftoff with a visionary or entrepreneurial project you've been trying to get off the ground. Need some advanced training or career coaching? This is an excellent time to sign up with the right person or institution.

July 25: Mars-Jupiter trine

It's not enough to bring home a paycheck. You'd like to know that, on some level, your work is making a difference in people's lives. Today, under this high-minded hookup, rally the troops around a shared goal. If your line of work is fulfilling but still leaves something to be desired, consider volunteering for an organization you admire.

July 29: Sun-Uranus square

Don't take the bait! Under this provocative face-off, someone may be testing you or just trying to push your buttons. Rather than react, get the upper hand by *not* engaging. And if this person happens to be a family member butting into your business, don't give them the satisfaction of seeing you upset. Just do your own thing without getting into an argument. Taurus for the win!

AUGUST: LOVE HOTSPOTS

August 2: Venus-Uranus square

When unpredictable Uranus in your sign squares tender Venus in your sensitive, sentimental fourth house, you may be prone to uncharacteristic emotional outbursts. Steer clear of people who are likely to push your buttons—but cozy up to those who always make you feel safe and loved.

August 7: Sun-Jupiter trine

This heart-opening angle gives you the optimism and confidence to wear your heart on your sleeve. You may need to let yourself be a little vulnerable, but that's how you build trust!

     The AstroTwins' 2019 Planetary Planner

August 8: Venus-Jupiter trine

Ready to go deeper? This expansive mashup gives your relationship mojo a booster shot. You may feel like it's finally time to take a next step toward long-term commitment—or renew your vows. Unattached but looking? Suit up and get back in the dating pool!

August 11-29: Mercury in Leo

After scuttling back and forth between Cancer and Leo, the messenger planet plunks down in your domestic fourth house for the next couple weeks. This is a stellar time to process any emotional issues that came up recently and find a way to discuss sensitive topics with your partner or a family member.

August 11: Jupiter retrograde ends

After four months of slowdowns and crossed wires, expansive Jupiter pivots back into forward motion in your eighth house of sex and intimacy. Bonds can deepen, or, if you've been wavering about a certain relationship, you'll have more clarity about how to proceed.

August 18-October 4: Mars in Virgo

Lusty Mars settles into your passionate fifth house for the next few weeks, dialing up your magnetism to peak levels. You can attract intriguing prospects or reboot the connection in your current relationship.

August 21-September 14: Venus in Virgo

Adding more heat to Mars' fire is the annual entrance of Venus into your fifth house of amour. Together, these cosmic lovebirds can't help but turn up the flames for some scorching late-summer romancing.

August 24: Venus-Mars meetup

This may be the hottest day of your 2019—regardless of what the mercury in your thermometer is reading! Fervent Mars only hooks up with sensual Venus once every other year, and this time around it happens to be in your lusty and glamorous fifth house. Enjoy!

August 26: Venus-Uranus trine

Some extra-spicy energy arrives with this anything-goes hookup of romantic Venus and unconventional Uranus in Taurus. Single? A casual convo can quickly develop into seductively flirty banter, which could lead to…who knows? Be prepared for anything, because that's exactly what you might get. Attached? Cue up a sexy surprise for tonight!

August 28: Mars-Uranus trine

Feeling a little claustrophobic? When passionate Mars sends a beam to liberated Uranus in your sign, you may crave more independence. If you've felt "trapped" in a relationship that no longer fits, here's your chance to break out. If, however, you just need to hit refresh, discuss it openly and land on terms that work for both of you. Single? You probably won't be playing for keeps tonight.

August 29-September 14: Mercury in Virgo

With loquacious Mercury cycling through your flirty and fun-loving fifth house, let the witty banter fly! Shift out of that overly practical mindset and you'll enjoy sparkling conversation and flirtatious interactions everywhere you turn.

August 30: Virgo new moon

This annual lunar lift in your passion zone opens you up to a promising love connection, possibly with someone from another background or culture. Set some intentions for romance and stay tuned in to your feelings. Take a gamble in the name of amour!

AUGUST: CAREER HOTSPOTS

August 11, 2019-January 11, 2020: Uranus retrograde in Taurus

The revolutionary planet begins its annual five-month backspin, this time around through your sign. It's a chance to step out of the spotlight and focus on a potential game-changing project. Use this slowdown to give your innovative ideas any necessary editing or revising.

August 11-29: Mercury in Leo

Mercury returns to Leo and your emotional fourth house for a second trip (retrograde-free, this time). If you lashed out at someone during a moody spell, make amends. A thwarted attempt to talk about your feelings or hash things out with family last month could go better now. Don't be surprised if you find yourself getting nostalgic and even weepy.

August 11: Jupiter retrograde ends

After four frustrating months of Jupiter backing through your power-player eighth house, the auspicious planet bolts back into forward motion and starts to sprinkle pixie dust in your realm of shared resources and joint ventures. If a partnership went through a rocky patch, you can go back to the bargaining table now and perhaps decide on even more favorable terms.

August 15: Aquarius full moon

This might be one of the most fateful days of the whole year for professional advancement! The only Aquarius full moon of 2019 signals a turning point or a moment of culmination of your past six months of hard work. As it lights up your tenth house of success, you could finally receive recognition for your talents and accomplishments. Accept it all with grace, but don't rest on your laurels. This is the perfect time to set your next round of intentions and hit the gas while the motor is revving.

August 16: Mercury-Uranus square

You're hyped up about an issue today but draw the line between being passionate and overly emotional. You may lose your audience if you get too dramatic or make it all about you.

August 18-October 4: Mars in Virgo

Lights, camera, Taurus! Ambitious Mars barrels into your creative and vivacious fifth house. Your talents could attract some fervent fans and with Mars in this attention-grabbing zone, your "audience engagement" might go through the roof. But don't do it for the accolades—take on a passion project that fulfills your soul. If others naturally gravitate to you because of it, that's just the cherry on top.

August 21: Mercury-Jupiter trine

You're thinking on a grand scale now, and people will be highly receptive to your ideas. When you approach them with confidence—and the data to back up your proposal—they'll be willing and even eager to take a leap of faith with you. Note: Your biggest supporters might be people from a very different background or industry than yours.

         The AstroTwins' 2019 Planetary Planner

August 29-September 14: Mercury in Virgo

Don't second-guess yourself! Dare to speak up boldly while expressive Mercury is in your confident and creative fifth house. Take the filters off and say what you feel in the moment instead of trying to please everyone with a political response.

August 29: Sun-Uranus trine

Uranus in your sign is shaking things up on a fundamental level, and when it fist-bumps the ego-driven Sun today, you'll be feeling fearless and empowered. If you simply *must* share something from your heart, do so. Just beware that your spontaneity might catch the other person off-guard. Be patient and give them a chance to process what you've just laid on them!

SEPTEMBER: LOVE HOTSPOTS

September 1: Venus-Saturn trine

Fantasies interrupted? Not to worry: You can get back to them later in the week. But today, as structured Saturn brings its unblinking clarity to a certain romantic situation, you'll actually be grateful for the reality check. Whether or not you're getting ready to take a pivotal step forward, you'll want to be sure you're not imagining anything.

September 1: Mercury-Uranus trine

When transformative Uranus pings the colorful communicator in your erotic eighth house, your mind will be overflowing with inventive ideas for behind-closed-doors activities. No partner on the radar? Look beyond the bar scene and same old dating apps, perhaps asking a friend for an introduction or showing up at cultural events that fascinate you.

September 2: Venus-Jupiter square

You may feel pulled in opposing directions under this uneasy cosmic clash. While the *idea* of a fling may sound appealing, you don't relish the prospect of post-game head games. Or, on the flip side, if you know you're going into this with a no-strings policy, you don't want to have to deal with an "emotional extraction" should the other party turn clingy. Attached? Jealousy could rise up out of nowhere, so try to keep your wits.

September 2: Sun-Mars meetup

Under this annual sync-up of the fearless Sun and passionate Mars in your lusty and sensual fifth house, you might be ready to take a risk and let someone know how you really feel. Why *not* make the first move? After all, nothing ventured, nothing gained!

September 3: Mercury-Mars meetup

You're all fired up to take a next step, but make sure you're not acting out of anxious or nervous energy. Get grounded before you talk to them, and you'll be irresistible under this dynamic duet!

September 4: Venus-Neptune opposition

Feelings may be strong—bordering on obsessive—today, but under Neptune's hazy halo, the object of your affections may be impossible to get a read on. Better to avoid doing anything extreme or irrevocable, if necessary by throwing yourself into a personal project or deep-cleaning mission.

September 6: Venus-Pluto trine

You could sense a potent connection with someone who seems to understand you without you even uttering a word. This person could hail from a different background or culture, but it won't matter one bit—you'll just "get" each other on a soul level. For couples, don't be afraid to wade into the deep end of the pool and share something vulnerable about your feelings and desires.

September 8: Sun-Jupiter square

You may be open to compromise on an emotional issue, but the other party might not be willing or able right now. Rather than push the issue—which will likely only backfire—try to get them to explain what's behind their resistance. If that's not possible, insist on "agreeing to disagree" and tabling this for another day.

September 13: Mercury-Venus meetup

When the love planet aligns with talkative Mercury in your amorous fifth house, you may just blurt out your feelings to your partner or drop the "L" word on a new romantic interest. That's your choice, but don't get upset if they can't respond in kind…yet.

September 14-October 8: Venus in Libra

When your celestial ruler, beautifying Venus, lands in your sixth house of wellness and self-care, you may find yourself at the juncture of fitness and romance. Attached? Suggest doing more active things together, like a fall hike or long bike ride. Single? Lose the earbuds. You might just strike up a conversation with an intriguing—and available—person at the gym or while out running errands. With Venus in this service-oriented sector, being helpful and supportive with each other will sweeten your bond.

September 25: Venus-Saturn square

Pump the brakes! Under this speed-checking transit, you may realize that a budding relationship is taking off a little too quickly or that you're not sure about someone's intentions for the future. Saturn can help you diplomatically downshift or, if you've been going *under* the speed limit, make a mindful move to the next level of closeness.

September 30: Venus-Pluto square

It'll be all too easy to focus on a love interest's flaws and foibles and get caught up in how you can "fix" them. That's a surefire route to frustration, so reset your GPS and retrain your vision on their positive qualities. Do they have enough of those to keep you satisfied? If the balance sheet keeps tipping the wrong way, you might have some serious rethinking to do.

SEPTEMBER: CAREER HOTSPOTS

September 5: Mercury-Saturn trine

Your mind is racing with innovative ideas, but if you need to bring something to a decision maker today, make sure you can back it up with solid facts and figures. Come prepared with a plan to explain this to the powers-that-be (and, if possible, how it can help *their* interests), and you'll be golden.

September 6: Mercury-Jupiter square

While honesty is generally the best policy, under this "too big to fail" face-off, you're better off saving your grand reveal for another day. You may be too far ahead of the curve with this, and while you hate to let the competition catch up, sometimes you simply have to wait for the perfect moment to strike.

September 6: Sun-Saturn trine

A smart risk could pay off big-time under this calculating mashup. Be prepared to pitch with necessary materials or a clear explanation of your concept. Need support or funding? Talk to your boss or that contact you made at an industry function who said to call them first with your next big idea. This could be it!

September 7: Mercury-Neptune opposition

Opinions: Everyone's got one, and soliciting too many will only serve to confuse you. While being a dictator isn't your goal, don't invite a fleet of chefs to season the broth, either. That will make the soup a murky mess!

September 8: Mercury-Pluto trine

Your mind is razor-sharp under this incisive alignment. You can read people like a book, *and* your intuition is dialed up to max levels. But don't take what anyone says at face value; pay attention to body language and other subtle cues.

September 8: Mars-Saturn trine

On this rare day when action planet Mars sweetly syncs up with structured Saturn, you'll be able to find the perfect pacing between racing ahead and taking it nice and slow. If you're considering a gamble, make sure it's a well-calculated one.

September 12: Mars-Jupiter square

Rein it in! A work project may have spiraled out of control, and now you need to scale it back. When you think about all the work involved, you might start to feel overwhelmed. But break it down into smaller, manageable steps. And if you've lost the vision that birthed this thing in the first place, trace the breadcrumbs or reread old emails to try to rekindle the spark.

September 13: Sun-Pluto trine

Let your power shine! With the bold Sun and profound Pluto in sync, your creative ideas could have a positive and far-reaching impact. Color outside the lines, even if others are afraid to take the risk. You'll lead by example—and soon, they'll want to follow suit.

September 14: Pisces full moon

The year's only full moon in your house of technology and teamwork may signal the celebratory completion to a long-running group project. Share the glory with your cohorts—and then with the rest of the world via social media. This isn't something to keep under wraps.

September 14: Mars-Neptune opposition

You've got so much energy you could bottle it, but make sure you're not spinning your wheels or headed toward a dead end. Mars pours rocket fuel in your tank, but dreamy Neptune can send you on a wild goose chase if you're not paying close attention.

September 14-October 3: Mercury in Libra

When thoughtful Mercury beams into beautifying Libra and your zone of health and self-care, the message is clear: Take care of numero uno before you tend to others! Stop procrastinating on those medical appointments. Get a massage on the books—better yet, buy a package. With mindful Mercury in your wellness zone, you might track your eating, sleep patterns and exercise, either with an app and Fitbit or just by jotting everything down in a small notebook. Experiment with healthy recipes (hello, harvest season) or get a couple trial passes to fitness studios that look interesting.

September 18: Saturn retrograde ends
If you've been twiddling your thumbs on a big idea since April 17, get ready to put those hands to more productive use. Today, structured Saturn helps you come up with a game plan to set this into motion. Calculated risks could pay off. You might resume efforts to launch a business, go back to school or publish something you're excited about.

September 19: Mars-Pluto trine
When assertive Mars in your creative fifth house fist-bumps alchemical Pluto in your zone of visionary thinking, you might hit on the perfect solution to a problem that's kept a team project in limbo. Run projections to make sure it can actually work, then pitch it to someone who can give it the green light.

September 21: Jupiter-Neptune square
Earth to Taurus! This rare mashup can make you uncharacteristically naïve and impractical. Don't let yourself get carried away with an idea that has zero chance of achieving liftoff. Force yourself to think on a way smaller, and more realistic, level—at least for now.

September 22: Mercury-Saturn square
Your sensible side is at war with the part of you that "dares to dream." Unfortunately, it looks like your skepticism has the advantage. Instead of scrapping all your creative plans, use this hardscrabble energy to your advantage: Find the weak spots or possible objections in your pitch, then work to strengthen those areas. Be careful about soliciting too many opinions because people could take the wind right out of your sails.

September 26: Mercury-Pluto square
While you may be sorely tempted to lash out or give someone an unedited piece of your mind, resist! Under these combustible skies, airing frustration will only churn up bad blood. Besides, you're not likely to get a clear answer out of anyone today. Lay low and wait it out.

September 28: Libra new moon
This once-a-year lunar lift powers up your efficient sixth house, helping you get a sprawling project back under control. And this is just the beginning! Over the coming six months, you can hit a big goal, but you need to get rid of the distractions and stay focused. Pro tip: Don't try to do it all yourself. Delegate what you can, and if you need even more hands on deck, invest in a service provider who specializes in this very thing.

OCTOBER: LOVE HOTSPOTS

October 3-December 9: Mercury in Scorpio
With the thoughtful planet traveling through your relationship realm, it's only natural for you to wonder where this thing is going. Mercury will

meander through here for an extra-long time, thanks to a retrograde from October 31 to November 20. Before that happens, make sure you have a clear understanding around your commitment or, if it's appropriate, an honest talk about the futures you both envision.

October 4-November 19: Mars in Libra

Watch for a critical, perfectionistic streak to flare during this temperamental transit, which only happens for a few weeks every two years. Couples could get stressed out and start to nitpick, but the last thing you want to do is take out your tensions on each other. Unattached? You might meet someone through fitness pursuits or volunteer work. Since the sixth house rules pets, leashing up your furry friend for a walk might put you in the path of a promising prospect. Hello, animal attraction!

October 8-November 1: Venus in Scorpio

When your ruler, charming Venus, joins Mercury in your partnership house, you may give serious thought to what you're hoping to draw into your life or how you want your current union to evolve. Putting just a little more effort into your dating strategies or communication style will pay off big-time.

October 12: Venus-Uranus opposition

Things could shift without much warning under this unpredictable showdown. But before you lose all sense of control, look at your role in a key relationship: Are you shape-shifting to fit into what *they* want? Compromise comes with the territory in successful relationships, but if you're living with resentment on a daily basis, it's time to get things out in the open.

October 13: Aries full moon

The year's only full moon in your twelfth house of endings and healing helps you leave a painful situation behind. No one says this is going to be easy, but if you really feel like it's time, call in some support and cut the cord. Write down your fears of letting go and ritualistically burn them. With la luna also igniting your fantasy fires, you might consummate a connection with a soulmate or let down those ironclad walls.

October 21: Venus-Neptune trine

Friends could become lovers today, as romantic Venus in your relationship realm unites with dreamy Neptune in your communal sector. Look no further than your current social circles for introductions, or just chat up new people while you're out and about. For couples, this is a great day to co-host a party (the more the merrier) or attend a festival or live show. With your eleventh house of activism lit up, doing a good deed could have a sweet boomerang effect. There's no better way to meet people—or strengthen an existing relationship—than through shared passions and commitments.

October 27: Scorpio new moon

The year's only new moon in your committed-partnership zone can help you write a new chapter in your personal book of love! If you're ready to turn over a new leaf—or plunge into a relationship with serious promise—take a risk. Set some intentions for a happy, healthy bond and read it daily until you manifest it. For duos who have gotten out of sync, this new moon helps you get back into a balanced groove.

TAURUS

OCTOBER: CAREER HOTSPOTS

October 3-December 9: Mercury in Scorpio

Eloquent Mercury spends an extended period in your partnership house, thanks to a retrograde from October 31 to November 20. Before and after those three weeks is an ideal time to hammer out a deal or negotiate the terms of a contract. Been on the outs with a colleague? Here's your chance to get back on the same page.

October 3: Pluto retrograde ends

Transformational Pluto wraps up a five-month retrograde in Capricorn and your risk-taking ninth house. If your optimism was dented, you'll regain your hopefulness now that Pluto is moving forward. Anything that stalled during that time can resume speed. Ventures with an entrepreneurial or educational twist are especially favored.

October 4-November 19: Mars in Libra

When the planet of motivation zips into your organized sixth house, you'll be stoked to get your professional life into lean, mean and efficient shape! Facing a complex, detailed project? Break it down into smaller chunks and set up a timeline to tackle them one by one. Pay close attention to your stress levels, since Mars here can ratchet up the tension.

October 7: Mercury-Uranus opposition

Hold your tongue! You may be burning to blurt out something that feels imperative to say, but speaking without thinking can create unnecessary chaos. Even constructive criticism will go over like a lead balloon. Write down your thoughts so you don't lose them, but wait until later in the week to decide whether or not to actually share them.

October 7: Sun-Saturn square

Facts may feel dull as dirt, but under this uber-practical mashup, they're your best friends. Some days are full of sexy, visionary projects, but on this one, you simply have to hunker down and do the grunt work.

October 14: Sun-Pluto square

If you see something, don't say something! Today, you may be the only one to notice that the emperor is wearing no clothes. But if everyone is invested in believing otherwise, don't be the one to upset the apple cart. Document your observations for (possible) future reference, but for now, keep them private.

October 15: Mercury-Neptune trine

Under today's sweet sync-up of your logical left brain (ruled by Mercury) and your imagination (Neptune's domain), your intuition will be just as reliable as a ream of spreadsheets. When you're this receptive, though, you need to shield your field. Your empathy is bordering on psychic levels, so be mindful that you don't absorb other people's energy and drain yourself.

October 27: Scorpio new moon

This annual lunation in your dynamic-duos zone could herald the beginning of a beautiful new partnership. But don't be so eager that you settle for less-than-equitable terms. If you're not completely happy with the whole offer, speak up. Be diplomatic but firm, and you're sure to reach a happy compromise.

 The AstroTwins' 2019 Planetary Planner

October 27: Mars-Saturn square

Go! Wait! It might be a day of mounting frustration as the action planet is body-checked by cautious Saturn. This could play out in the form of somebody who is trying to micromanage you or who's hung up on protocol and procedure. Lean in to your sign's trademark patience, and when you feel like you're at the end of your rope, turn your attention to something you have more control over.

October 28: Sun-Uranus opposition

There's a time to own your talents and accomplishments and a time to fade into the background and wear your team-player uniform. Today, you need to do more of the latter, as any form of grandstanding will read as arrogant or self-interested.

October 31-November 20: Mercury retrograde in Scorpio

The communicator planet backflips into your partnership house for three weeks, which could delay a deal or collaboration you were hoping to ink before Thanksgiving. Patience is a virtue, even if it does raise your blood pressure by a dozen points.

NOVEMBER: LOVE HOTSPOTS

November 1-25: Venus in Sagittarius

November might be one for the romantic record books as vixen Venus parades through your seductive eighth house and turns up the heat. Chemistry could ignite for single Bulls, and couples may be ready for that next big step, whether that means exchanging house keys, an engagement or a pregnancy.

November 14: Venus-Neptune square

Fantasy can inspire deeper connection, but if it's not based on anything real, you might wind up with an aching heart. If you catch yourself about to tumble down a deep, dark rabbit hole, find out whether this person feels anything for you. Be doubly wary about online affairs. It's easy to hide behind a couple of photos and empty words. You need something you can take to the bank.

November 19-January 3: Mars in Scorpio

When the red-blooded planet scorches into your relationship house, it can bring sexy back for couples and point the way to serious prospects for single Bulls. You'll turn heads wherever you go, which is flattering, but make sure you're at least somewhat interested before you take the bait.

November 20: Mercury retrograde ends

Breathe a sigh of relief as the messenger planet gets back on track and gives your relationship a reboot! The tension in a serious union may have reached epic proportions over the past few weeks, but now you can get on the same page or move forward with a clear conscience.

November 24: Mars-Uranus opposition

This one-day combustible confab can spark volcanic tempers and lead to angry outbursts. You might act out competitively with your partner or crush. Of course, if you're both willing to forgive and forget, you could be in for some sizzling makeup sex!

November 24: Venus-Jupiter meetup

The two "benefics" only meet up once a year, and it can be 12 years in between their trysts in your intense eighth house. Today's rendezvous may open you up to new adventures in sex, emotion and connection. Keep a metaphoric fire extinguisher close at hand: This could get hot.

November 25-December 20: Venus in Capricorn

Romantic Venus sails into your ninth house of travel, expansion and long-distance love for its second visit this year. Sparks could fly with someone from another culture, or you might strike up conversation with a fellow holiday season traveler. Couples looking for the perfect gift (or making a wish list of your own) should check out hotel and airfare deals.

November 26: Sagittarius new moon

There's only one of these new moons in your eighth house of eroticism and intimacy a year, and this one can deepen your current bond or attract a different kind of person into your orbit. But in the sign of the uber-candid Archer, la luna requires you to get vulnerable and even more honest—with other people, but mainly with yourself. Is there something you're afraid to admit? Take a risk and see what happens when you drop your guard.

November 28: Venus-Uranus trine

Don't apologize if you're contentedly single! It's 2019, and there are no rules about how to conduct your love life. That said, if you're more of the commitment type, seek what's truly in your heart or, if you're attached, make sure you're getting your needs met.

NOVEMBER: CAREER HOTSPOTS

November 5: Mars-Pluto square

Aggro Mars in your micromanaging sixth house clashes with intensifier Pluto. Small things can conflate into epic conflicts, so come to the table prepared to compromise on a key point. While you don't want to totally abandon your mission, stay open to the fact that someone might actually know a better way to accomplish it.

November 8: Sun-Neptune trine

This is a great day for networking with people outside your usual camp. You might discover that someone you thought of as a competitor is actually in alignment with your highest values. Drop your swords and team up FTW!

November 12: Taurus full moon

The year's only full moon in your sign is like a birthday present and curtain call rolled into one. You'll earn some much-deserved kudos for your efforts of the past six months, so don't make them come find you. Step out from the shadows and assume your place on the main stage. Take a bow, then get busy formulating your next big set of goals!

November 13: Mercury-Neptune trine

With analytical Mercury spinning retrograde *and* connected to sensitive Neptune, your intuition is a reliable guide. If you have an old conflict to resolve, bring your most compassionate A-game and bury this hatchet once and for all.

November 19-January 3: Mars in Scorpio

Driven Mars in your house of strategic alliances sets the stage for some successful and fast-paced dynamic duos. The red planet will stoke your competitive nature, giving you the upper hand when it comes to deal-brokering or negotiating.

November 20: Mercury retrograde ends

You can hit the refresh button on a collaborative project that stalled when the messenger planet turned retrograde on Halloween. The tension is no longer palpably mounting, and now all parties will be ready to pick up where you left off—and blast ahead!

November 24: Mars-Uranus opposition

Competition may be unavoidable under today's uneasy face-off of these hotheaded planets. No one's willing to give an inch, yet everyone's quick to point the finger. If you sense that trying to work it out is an exercise in futility, table it for another day.

November 26: Sagittarius new moon

The year's only new moon in your house of shared resources and joint ventures plants seeds for mutually beneficial long-term investments. If you get itchy feet, remind yourself that you're in this for the long haul. It's worth your while to research thoroughly first.

November 27: Neptune retrograde ends

When nebulous Neptune ends a five-month retrograde in your eleventh house of teamwork and technology, the fog lifts and you'll clearly see who's been pulling their share of the load and who's been slacking. Jettison the dead weight and assemble your dream team.

DECEMBER: LOVE HOTSPOTS

December 9-28: Mercury in Sagittarius

Casual might turn to *committed* quickly under this intensifying cycle. With mental Mercury parked in your intimate eighth house, you may not be happy with just an on-off relationship. Since Mercury gets conversation flowing, you'll be able to express some of these thoughts, as well as a couple secret desires and fantasies. The holidays just got hotter!

December 11: Venus-Saturn meetup

Long-range Saturn syncs up with the love planet, prompting you to question what you really want for the future. Venus helps you speak honestly and diplomatically about your hopes and dreams. For some Bulls, a long-distance connection could turn serious.

December 13: Mars-Neptune trine

Sexual chemistry could erupt with someone you consider a friend or with an online match that you weren't expecting much from. Neptune opens you up emotionally—but it can also blur the facts. Enjoy the ride, but keep at least one eye on where things are headed. Couples may be inspired to try something experimental and new.

December 13: Venus-Pluto meetup

There's no dodging the truth today as amorous Venus merges with probing Pluto in your candid ninth house. It's important to speak from the heart—but equally vital that you listen with both ears.

December 20-January 13: Venus in Aquarius

When vivacious Venus veers in your career corner, you may be spending more time at the office. For couples, this could throw a wrench in some together-time, so prepare in advance by planning a special makeup date or two. Single? Dress for success *and* to impress. Intriguing prospects could be hanging out at industry events or even on your after-work train commute.

December 22: Venus-Uranus square

Commitment or freedom? The two may be hard to reconcile under this air-sucking angle. Uranus is all about independence and self-expression, which can send a jolt of tension through a solid or budding relationship. You don't have to bolt, but you should honestly discuss any desires to go "off-leash."

DECEMBER: CAREER HOTSPOTS

December 2, 2019-December 19, 2020: Jupiter in Capricorn

A new day—make that year—dawns as expansive Jupiter wraps up its 13-month residency in Sagittarius and your house of intimacy and shared resources. For the next year, the planet of luck will traipse through Capricorn and your ninth house of entrepreneurship, education and travel. Take your gap year if you've planned well enough, but note that Capricorn is not "capricious." Any risks you take need to be heavily researched—and safely hedged. But once that's done, you're free to go exploring!

December 8: Sun-Neptune square

Guard your intellectual property and treat it like the treasure it is! People may be talking a good game, but nebulous Neptune can distort reality. This is a better day for brainstorming and big-picture thinking. Trying to nail down details will be a waste of time, because more info is likely to come to light. Keep things open-ended for now.

December 9-28: Mercury in Sagittarius

Hunker down and research! With mental Mercury in your investigative eighth house for the next couple weeks, the divine is in the details. You may be a bit more private or focused, as a captivating idea could bring you to near-obsessive levels. Watch for too much tunnel vision but do capitalize on your ramped-up powers of concentration. There's a lot you can accomplish before everyone clocks out for the holidays so filter those distractions!

December 12: Gemini full moon

This annual event that illuminates your second house of work, security and money can indicate the successful completion of a long-running project or the maturity of a smart financial move. You could see an immediate bump in your income, but it might take up to six months to materialize. Either way, you're moving into a new level of prosperity. If you're a newbie at investing, talk to a few different pros to learn the basics and assess your own comfort level with risk.

December 13: Mars-Neptune trine

Networking could open some serendipitous doors today. You don't have to reinvent the wheel if a friend or colleague has a whole shop full of them. Talk to people about potential opportunities and be direct about your skills and what you're looking for. An inspiring contact may open your eyes to new possibilities or offer to join forces. This rare sync-up bodes well for collaborative work, especially anything with a humanitarian or activist platform.

December 15: Jupiter-Uranus trine

This is a perfect day to make a bold move or to take a huge risk. With lucky Jupiter fist-bumping wild-card Uranus, you might catch people so off-guard that they can't come up with a good reason to say no. Because these two powerhouses are in grounded earth signs, your big idea is probably viable—and it's certainly original!

December 19: Mercury-Neptune square

You're chomping at the bit to get a new initiative off the ground, but hazy Neptune is making it impossible to get the info you need to move forward. Pushing or cajoling won't help. Better to set it aside for the moment and wait another day or so for the fog to lift.

December 20-January 13: Venus in Aquarius

Hoping to make a professional change? With amiable Venus taking up residence in your career corner for the next three weeks, get out and mingle for your jingle. Keep your bag stocked with business cards and your elevator pitch at the ready! Need some new marketing material? This is the perfect time for headshots, a website and social media update or a brand refresh.

December 26: Capricorn new moon (solar eclipse)

This annual event—and the second Capricorn new moon of 2019—can help a big dream achieve liftoff. If you've been kicking this around for much of the year, stop thinking and take concrete action. You may have to take a risk to pull this off, but remember, you've got support from both seen and unseen sources. This uplifting new moon happens to be an annular solar eclipse, a rare event also known as the "ring of fire," which will heat up your plans in a big way!

December 27: Sun-Jupiter meetup

This just might be the luckiest day of the year, as the two most confident and expansive planets merge in your house of visionary thinking. If you allow yourself to dream big and work to eliminate all self-imposed limits, you can break through a huge barrier. This globally galvanizing meetup might inspire you to plan an exciting trip or get serious about that entrepreneurial venture!

December 28-January 16: Mercury in Capricorn

When the messenger planet alights in your expansive ninth house, you'll find inspiration outside your comfort zone, which will come in especially handy if you've hit a creative plateau. Almost anything (or anywhere) unfamiliar is a good place to start. Wander through galleries and museums, take a day trip, skip the small talk and share some of your loftiest ideas. Sign up for a workshop to get the year off to a stimulating start!

December 30: Mercury-Uranus trine

This galvanizing alignment can inspire you to think outside the box with your New Year's resolutions. Radical honesty can revolutionize everything, but before you blurt out the first thing that pops into your head, take an honest look at your needs and desires as the year closes out and find a non-confrontational way to express them. ✳

2019

NUMEROLOGY

3

THE 3 UNIVERSAL YEAR

By Felicia Bender

THE PRACTICAL NUMEROLOGIST

THE 3 UNIVERSAL YEAR

Make connections! A year of creativity and self-expression awaits.

In numerology, each calendar year adds up to a single-digit number, which resonates at a unique vibration. We all feel this energy, and it's called the Universal Year.

A Universal Year means that everyone on the planet will experience the frequency of a particular number during the entire year, from January 1 until December 31.

Whether or not you make New Year's resolutions, most of us intuitively feel a profound energy shift whenever the calendar turns. In numerology, that transition is a big deal, marking the passage into a new Universal Year—the shared atmosphere of the world for a 12-month period.

You can think of the Universal Year as the state or country you're driving through on your yearly "road trip." The Universal Year number will set the GPS and chart our collective course.

Where We're Coming From

The progression of Universal Years from 1 to 9 is a complete journey, so we look at the surrounding years to see where we're coming from and where we're headed. In 2017, which was a 1 Universal Year, we began a whole new cycle—and the world certainly reflected that.

Next, 2018 was a Master 11/2 Universal Year. Master numbers are repeating numbers like 11, 22 and 33, which create a secondary vibration, giving the year an infusion of paradox and power. These numbers carry a higher frequency and demand evolution.

Last year's Universal energy brought a higher spiritual purpose to the planet, and also ramped up the intensity. We were pulled between the

How to Calculate the Universal Year:

Add the individual numbers of the current year together, like this:

$$2019 = 2 + 0 + 1 + 9 = 12$$

Then reduce again:

$$1 + 2 = 3$$

2019 is a 3 Universal Year

All of us will begin to feel this energy starting January 1, 2019 and the effect will end on December 31, 2019.

cooperation, or at least with mutual respect. However successful we were with that mission, either globally *or* locally, it became clear that we had to rise above the divisiveness that's been destroying our world.

While the energy and events of 2018 are still impacting us, a shift in perspective is coming our way. 2019 offers up a reconfiguration of our core sense of reality and our place within it. That's no small feat. And that change won't happen overnight or in one 12-month cycle of time. In fact, each time a Universal Year rings in, it begins a whole new cycle until that same Universal Year number returns a decade later.

The 3 Universal Year

The number 3 in numerology is the vibration of creative self-expression and emotional sensitivity. It emanates joy, optimism, social engagement and communication. Universally, we're being offered energy that supports infusing creativity, fun and connection into all that we do. Humor and lightness hold immense power and can help us face any heaviness or monumental change.

This year will help us take the spiritual illumination initiated by 2018 and infuse it into a newfound sense of purpose and power.

The most enlightened use of the number 3 is to inspire and uplift others. This Universal Year is set up as a blank canvas awaiting our most meaningful contributions. The mantra for the 3 Universal Year is to *speak your truth*. But in order to do so, you have

diplomatic "2" energy of love, patience, and cooperation, while also navigating a double dose of the contrasting "1" energy, which emphasizes individuality, taking initiative and flying solo.

As a result, it was a year of oppositions that heightened feeling of division and polarity: us/them, love/hate, war/peace material/spiritual. While that was tough to navigate, the more "enlightened" mission was to discover our collective responsibility—to ourselves and each other.

The balancing beams of the 11/2 Universal Year called on us to start working in harmonious to know what your "truth" even is—and (hint) it's not just an uninformed opinion or knee-jerk reaction to the latest headlines.

And that's where it gets tricky: How do we hold on to our own truth while allowing others to have theirs? How do we express our beliefs and stand up for ourselves when our values don't align with someone else's? How do we discern the difference between "truth" and "values"? Or "truth" and "integrity"? Or "truth" and "dogma"?

Author Byron Katie, who teaches a self-inquiry method called The Work, suggests that beliefs are just thoughts we think over and over again. When we change our thoughts, we change our beliefs. Katie's method involves asking yourself these four questions, especially if something that's become a fixed belief, or "truth," in your head is causing you to suffer:

Is it true?

Can you absolutely know it's true?

How do you react—what happens—when you believe that thought?

Who would you be without this thought?

It seems the first step in this 3 Universal Year is to reflect on what we've adopted as the truth before speaking, typing or posting a word. The seemingly simple act of "speaking your truth" turns out not to be so simple after all. It's a layered process, and one we'll all be supported in exploring in 2019: Connecting with our individual, and then collective, truth—and expressing it in a healthy, respectful and transformative way.

3 is the number of creation and this is an extremely fertile year for all forms of creativity. In addition to novel problem-solving, scientific and medical innovation, and new environmental solutions, the 3 Universal Year highlights the arts as a conduit for expression on all levels. We have seen how artistic communities have stepped forward and used their influence to speak out about everything from global warming to saying, "Time's Up!" to sexual predators and gender discrimination. This influence will gain even more velocity and power in 2019.

How to Step into The Creative Power of the 3 Universal Year
Practice impeccable communication.

The energy of the year demands that we brush up on our communication skills across the board. This holds true for our most intimate relationships, extends to the way we express ourselves at work, and bleeds over into all our engagements, large and small. How do you speak to yourself? What's your internal dialogue? Is it true, kind and constructive? How do you speak to your friends and family? Are you able to "be yourself" no matter what your surroundings? How do you speak to the person working the drive-through or to the barista who makes your coffee? This is a time to truly choose your words with mindful precision. When in doubt, listen twice as much as you speak.

Lighten up and see new possibilities.

The gift of the number 3 is its bright light of fun, wit and humor. Think about it: Do we learn the most when the task is serious and punishing? Or do we aborb more when the lesson feels like play—when we laugh along the way, and feel supported and validated as we make mistakes *and* as we succeed?

Intelligent and curious, the 3 thrives when delving into the depths of expression, spinning the old into something novel and fresh. Before you throw out the baby with the bathwater, see if you can salvage or reinvent a situation. The best use of a 3 Universal Year is to take existing ideas and concepts and "upcycle" them. Create new twists on services and products to make them into something fresh and relevant that serves the greater good. The 3 Universal Year opens us up to new ideas, and challenges us to also inspire others along the way.

Learn something new.

2019 is the year to "upgrade thyself." No more driving in the same ruts in the road. Mentally, physically and spiritually, the 3 Universal Year encourages us to go boldly into new and improved terrain. Treat life like an adventure! The magic manifests when we infuse a sense of joy and optimism into everything we do. This will build on the independence and individuality we've gained over the last two Universal Years. Take the independence of the 1 Year (and last year's

Master number 11), grab a buddy as a nod to the 2 Year's cooperative vibe, and head off on that unchartered mission. You'll thrive when you give new experiences a go!

Challenges of the 3 Universal Year
Manage your emotions.

One of the issues with the energy of the number 3 is that it brings *all* of our emotions to the table—the good, the bad and the ugly—not to mention the known, unknown and repressed. The 3 Universal Year demands that we get real and responsible about our feelings. The year will be full of global trigger points, and it will demand higher levels of self-awareness so that we're not all walking around raging and reacting to everything that pushes our buttons.

As the saying goes, feelings are not facts. But for some people, the energy of the 3 will bring choppy emotional waves that can translate into depressive or melancholy moments. It would be a good time to revisit Eckhardt Tolle's *The Power of Now*, which teaches us how to become observers of our thoughts and feelings, rather than getting caught up in their maelstrom. That may require being vigilant about the conversations we have and the thoughts we simply accept at face value, ones that trigger a whole cascade of brain chemicals and reactions.

The film *What the Bleep Do We Know?* gives a fascinating look at the neuroscience behind our emotional reactions. Well worth watching!

       The AstroTwins' 2019 Planetary Planner

Stick it out—you've got this!

As buoyant as 3 energy can be, it can also provoke severe moments of self-doubt that cause us to waver in our commitments. The 3 can be scattered—and this year, we may find ourselves starting lots of projects and losing steam before we finish. Watch out for a distracting case of Shiny Object Syndrome. During a 3 Universal Year we can all benefit from gentle focus and active follow-through. Consider putting a "Pomodoro timer" app on your smartphone to help you work in focused bursts or teaming up with an accountability partner to help you stay on track.

Think before you speak.

It'll be a challenge to not only watch our words (while speaking "authentically,"), but also to bring precision to the way we communicate. That means: Choosing the proper words. Choosing not to gossip or tear others apart with sarcasm and hurtful snipes. Choosing to get more in touch with our truth—and to speak it with consistency and grace.

The Big Picture

Overall, the 3 Universal Year shines a spotlight on creative self-expression, joy, optimism and authentic communication. The year brings opportunities to express new ideas and discover novel approaches to broken systems. It's earmarked for all of us to take an honest look at how we express our feelings, desires and fears.

Despite deep unrest we feel on a global scale, the universal energy for 2019 invites us into the sandbox, onto the stage and into the spotlight. It reminds us to play and laugh, to find lightness in the shadows and to shine our light into the dark crevices in order to bring creative solutions to the planet. ✳

Felicia Bender, Ph.D. (The Practical Numerologist) is Astrostyle's resident numerologist and author of *Redesign Your Life: Using Numerology to Create the Wildly Optimal You* and *Master Numbers 11, 22, and 33: The Ultimate Guide.* Follow her at www.FeliciaBender.com.

2019
CHINESE HOROSCOPE

YEAR OF THE EARTH PIG

YEAR OF THE EARTH PIG

In Chinese astrology, the pleasure-loving, sociable Earth Pig will reign from February 5, 2019, until January 25, 2020.

Come on out of the doghouse—there's a party in the pen! As we celebrate the Chinese (Lunar) New Year this February 5, 2019, the Year of the Earth Pig begins, kicking off the night before with the Lunar New Year's Eve on February 4. After two intense years, this convivial cycle gives us a chance to "rest and digest." The pregnant pause of 2019 might even help us make some sense of all the global mudslinging that's been going around. Serenity now?

The pleasant and genial Earth Pig's arrival will be a welcome relief after 2018's Earth Dog antics. Dogs are pack animals, and in the past year, groups have stuck together out of "loyalty," at times, to a fault. It's widely agreed that the world has never felt more divided, and no surprise that the coop-stalking energy of 2017's Rooster and the border-guarding vibes of 2018's Dog spiraled into xenophobic extremes. To wit, hate crimes have increased internationally and last year saw the tragic separation of children from parents who were seeking asylum at the U.S. border.

Reinstate that open-door policy! The Earth Pig's M.O. is far more welcoming. This friendly creature can be quite the social butterfly, with pals from all walks of life. In 2019, a good bottle of vino—not a good fence—makes a good neighbor. (From #WineTime to #SwineTime?)

Pigs are complex communicators who dream, recognize their own names and have over twenty oinks and squeaks that have been identified with an actual language that they share. Some scientists believe that their social skills rival those of primates. Unlike the territorial animals who governed 2017 and 2018, Rooster and Dog, the easygoing Pig cohabitates well with other barnyard species. Perhaps 2019 will be the year where people start engaging in legitimate dialogues again, instead of simply barking at each through the "picture window" of social media.

During the Earth Dog's tenure in 2018, our homes were our shelters. Many people spent a pretty penny on décor and tucked away in their comfy nests. But what's the fun of splurging on the hand-loomed textiles and thrown-ceramic dishes if you can't show them off to guests? Cocktail parties will be de rigueur again in 2019, with a rainbow coalition of guests in attendance. We might even resume "dressing for dinner," instead of rocking the athleisure at five-star venues.

Forget what you heard about a messy room being a "pigsty" or people "sweating like pigs." While real-world swines roll around in mud to cool off, they are clean creatures by nature. In the year ahead, our spaces may become a lot more orderly and neat. No leaving dishes stacked up by the sink for days

The AstroTwins' 2019 Planetary Planner

after those soirees—or indulging in excess plastic packaging that winds up floating in the oceans and being digested by fish. (Scary!) Cleanliness is next to godliness during the Earth Pig year. That said, Pigs are known for having their lazy spells. This might be the year to hire a housekeeper for a regular deep clean, especially if you're the type who "doesn't do windows."

Who do you call a friend? Alas, the Earth Pig isn't always the most discerning creature. In 2019, guilt by association can be an issue for folks who naively get caught up with the wrong crowd. Mingling at the pub and exchanging pleasantries with friendly acquaintances? That's one thing. But before declaring anyone "squad," make sure you know their true background. Are they playing dirty behind the scenes? Appearances can be deceiving during the Year of the Earth Pig. Bottom line: Don't let other people wipe their mud on your clean reputation and sully your name.

When it comes to love, the Earth Pig isn't exactly the most romantic creature. In 2019, we may have to work a little harder to cultivate the sexy sparks. That said, the Pig is associated with Scorpio in the Western zodiac, and it's certainly possible to bring out our "wild boars" in the bedroom. (Easy with those tusks, please.) Like Scorpio, the Pig is a water sign in the Chinese zodiac—capable of deep and powerful emotion. And yet, the intensity of those feelings might be a big much for people to bear,

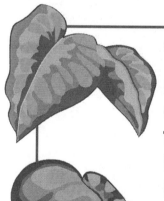

What's Your Chinese Zodiac Sign?

Rat: 1924, 1936, 1948, 1960, 1972, 1984, 1996, 2008
Ox: 1925, 1937, 1949, 1961, 1973, 1985, 1997, 2009
Tiger: 1926, 1938, 1950, 1962, 1974, 1986, 1998, 2010
Rabbit: 1927, 1939, 1951, 1963, 1975, 1987, 1999, 2011
Dragon: 1928, 1940, 1952, 1964, 1976, 1988, 2000, 2012
Snake: 1929, 1941, 1953, 1965, 1977, 1989, 2001, 2013
Horse: 1930, 1942, 1954, 1966, 1978, 1990, 2002, 2014
Sheep: 1931, 1943, 1955, 1967, 1979, 1991, 2003, 2015
Monkey: 1932, 1944, 1956, 1968, 1980, 1992, 2004, 2016
Rooster: 1933, 1945, 1957, 1969, 1981, 1993, 2005, 2017
Dog: 1934, 1946, 1958, 1970, 1982, 1994, 2006, 2019
Pig: 1935, 1947, 1959, 1971, 1983, 1995, 2007, 2019

YEAR OF THE PIG

especially with the grounded Earth energy ruling this year. No need to process every trauma all at once in 2019; just deal in small and therapeutic kilobytes. And don't forget that fun and laughter can be anti-depressants, too.

The last time we had an Earth Pig year was 1959. On the surface, it was an uneventful period in history— despite Fidel Castro coming into power on February 16, the grand finale to 1958's Alpha-empowering Earth Dog cycle. But a few key developments emerged under the Earth Pig's tenure. The microchip was invented, which is the foundation of the Digital Age in which we now live. Research officially began on the birth-control pill and Alaska and Hawaii became the 49th and 50th states—a nod to the Earth Pig's inclusive diplomacy. The Barbie doll was introduced to the world in 1959, an unwitting symbol of the "plastic is fantastic" superficiality that can mark an Earth Pig year. And, the ribbon was cut on the visually arresting Guggenheim Museum in New York City, which houses many modern and "eccentric" works of art.

Interestingly, on July 24, 1959, then-Vice President Richard Nixon got swept into the famous "kitchen debate" with Soviet Premier Nikita Khrushchev. During an exhibition that was meant to foster cultural exchange between the U.S. and Russia, the gloves came off as the two leaders began a verbal battle about capitalism versus communism.

> **"Financially, the Earth Pig has a solid work ethic and is willing to put in the long hours to get ahead."**

The finger-pointing drama took place in a model kitchen that was set up as part of the exhibit as Nixon suggested that Khrushchev's threats of using nuclear power could lead to war. In the end—and in true Earth Pig style—both leaders pulled back from the debate and claimed a desire for peace. With U.S. and Russian relations see-sawing wildly after proven election hacking and unprecedented summits, it will be interesting to see what this Earth Pig year brings.

Health-wise, Earth Pig years are times where we might have to monitor our diets more carefully. It's easy to overdo it on the sweets and rich foods. (And watch that "liquid courage"!) Gentler forms of exercise like hiking and swimming are favored—and sleep sanctity should be honored in the name of keeping our immune systems strong.

Financially, the Earth Pig is slowly, but steadily, abundant. This zodiac sign has a solid work ethic and is willing to put in the hours to get ahead. Patience and willpower are the name of the game for anyone wishing to get ahead in 2019. And don't forget the power of building friendly alliances with colleagues. Pigs are often the office optimists and motivators; the ones who will keep the team spirit burning bright.

Want to mark yourself as a rising star? In addition to delivering solid work in 2019, be the "crew glue" of your coworkers, rallying everyone for a company picnic or happy hour and keeping the momentum

 The AstroTwins' 2019 Planetary Planner

strong. Where Pigs can fall short is in setting clear-cut goals and a solid schedule. Work harder to implement those project management systems and you'll be sure to succeed in 2019.

On a global level, employment will be a hot topic of discussion. Creating (and retaining) jobs will be an important mission for many countries, which may require some fancy economic footwork. Since people will be out and about more often, 2019 could bring a boon for the hospitality, fashion and entertainment industries. While the Earth Pig certainly doesn't mind a powerful title, this is not necessarily a super-ambitious year. Quality of life is as important as a paycheck and some people may decide that a slower pace is more fulfilling than endlessly climbing the corporate ladder.

Money management may be a struggle in 2019. The indulgent Earth Pig loves fine food, vintage bubbles and elegant fashion house finds. Under this feel-good spell, there will be days when we might just want to buy a round of champagne for an entire bar of strangers. Fun, fun, fun...but what about the funds? In 2019, we'll have to be careful not to burn as fast as we earn.

To avoid such slips, it would be wise to create a set-and-forget financial plan. Activate the auto-pay features for your monthly utilities or have money transferred into savings and investment accounts. If you don't see it, you won't spend it. Just make sure you also create an entertainment fund!

2019
COSMIC
CALENDAR

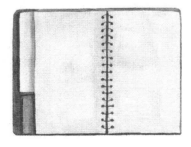

DAILY
PLANETARY GUIDE

 The AstroTwins' 2019 Planetary Planner

January 2019

	MONDAY
1	TUESDAY
2	WEDNESDAY
3	THURSDAY
4 ☿ Mercury enters Capricorn	FRIDAY
5 ♑ Capricorn new moon (partial solar eclipse) ●	SATURDAY
6 ♈ Uranus retrograde in Aries	SUNDAY

92

January 2019

7 ♀ Venus enters Sagittarius — MONDAY

8 — TUESDAY

9 — WEDNESDAY

10 — THURSDAY

11 — FRIDAY

12 — SATURDAY

13 Waxing quarter moon in Aries ☽ — SUNDAY

         The AstroTwins' 2019 Planetary Planner

January 2019

14	MONDAY
15	TUESDAY
16	WEDNESDAY
17	THURSDAY
18	FRIDAY
19	SATURDAY
20 ≈ Sun enters Aquarius	SUNDAY

94

January 2019

21 ♌ Leo full moon (total lunar eclipse & supermoon) ○   MONDAY

22   TUESDAY

23   WEDNESDAY

24 ☿ Mercury enters Aquarius   THURSDAY

25   FRIDAY

26   SATURDAY

27 Waning quarter moon in Scorpio ◑   SUNDAY

          The AstroTwins' 2019 Planetary Planner

January 2019

28	MONDAY
29	TUESDAY
30	WEDNESDAY
31	THURSDAY
	FRIDAY
	SATURDAY
	SUNDAY

February 2019

MONDAY

TUESDAY

WEDNESDAY

THURSDAY

1   FRIDAY

2   SATURDAY

3 ♀ **Venus enters Capricorn**   SUNDAY

February 2019

---

4 ♒ Aquarius new moon ●   MONDAY

---

5 Chinese New Year (Earth Pig)   TUESDAY

---

6   WEDNESDAY

---

7   THURSDAY

---

8   FRIDAY

---

9   SATURDAY

---

10 ☿ Mercury enters Pisces   SUNDAY

February 2019

11 ———————————————————————————— MONDAY

12 ———————————————————————————— TUESDAY
Waxing quarter moon in Taurus ☽

13 ———————————————————————————— WEDNESDAY

14 ———————————————————————————— THURSDAY
♂ **Mars enters Taurus**

15 ———————————————————————————— FRIDAY

16 ———————————————————————————— SATURDAY

17 ———————————————————————————— SUNDAY

 The AstroTwins' 2019 Planetary Planner

February 2019

| 18 | ♓ Sun enters Pisces | MONDAY |

| 19 | ♍ Virgo full moon (supermoon) ○ | TUESDAY |

| 20 | | WEDNESDAY |

| 21 | | THURSDAY |

| 22 | | FRIDAY |

| 23 | | SATURDAY |

| 24 | | SUNDAY |

February 2019

25   MONDAY

26   TUESDAY
Waning quarter moon in Sagittarius ◑

27   WEDNESDAY

28   THURSDAY

FRIDAY

SATURDAY

SUNDAY

The AstroTwins' 2019 Planetary Planner

March 2019

MONDAY

TUESDAY

WEDNESDAY

THURSDAY

1 ♀ **Venus enters Aquarius**   FRIDAY

2   SATURDAY

3   SUNDAY

March 2019

4   MONDAY

5   ☿ Mercury retrograde in Pisces   TUESDAY

6   ♓ Pisces new moon ●   WEDNESDAY
    ♅ Uranus enters Taurus

7   THURSDAY

8   FRIDAY

9   SATURDAY

10   SUNDAY

                The AstroTwins' 2019 Planetary Planner

March 2019

11 ─────────────────────────────────
MONDAY

12 ─────────────────────────────────
TUESDAY

13 ─────────────────────────────────
WEDNESDAY

14 Waxing quarter moon in Gemini ◑
THURSDAY

15 ─────────────────────────────────
FRIDAY

16 ─────────────────────────────────
SATURDAY

17 ─────────────────────────────────
SUNDAY

March 2019

18	MONDAY

19	TUESDAY

20 ♈ Sun enters Aries ♎ Libra full moon	WEDNESDAY

21	THURSDAY

22	FRIDAY

23	SATURDAY

24	SUNDAY

March 2019

25 ──────────────────────────────── MONDAY

26 ──────────────────────────────── TUESDAY
♀ Venus enters Pisces

27 ──────────────────────────────── WEDNESDAY

28 ──────────────────────────────── THURSDAY
☿ Mercury retrograde ends
Waning quarter moon in Capricorn ◑

29 ──────────────────────────────── FRIDAY

30 ──────────────────────────────── SATURDAY

31 ──────────────────────────────── SUNDAY
♂ Mars enters Gemini

The AstroTwins' 2019 Planetary Planner   106

April 2019

1 _____ MONDAY

2 _____ TUESDAY

3 _____ WEDNESDAY

4 _____ THURSDAY

5 ♈ Aries new moon ● _____ FRIDAY

6 _____ SATURDAY

7 _____ SUNDAY

 The AstroTwins' 2019 Planetary Planner

April 2019

| 8 | MONDAY |

| 9 | TUESDAY |

| 10 | ♃ Jupiter retrograde in Sagittarius | WEDNESDAY |

| 11 | THURSDAY |

| 12 | Waxing quarter moon in Cancer ◑ | FRIDAY |

| 13 | SATURDAY |

| 14 | SUNDAY |

April 2019

15	MONDAY

16	TUESDAY

17	WEDNESDAY

☿ **Mercury enters Aries**

18	THURSDAY

19	FRIDAY

♎ Libra full moon ○

20	SATURDAY

♉ Sun enters Taurus
♀ **Venus enters Aries**

21	SUNDAY

April 2019

22	MONDAY
23	TUESDAY
24 ♇ Pluto retrograde in Capricorn	WEDNESDAY
25	THURSDAY
26 Waning quarter moon in Aquarius ◑	FRIDAY
27	SATURDAY
28	SUNDAY

April 2019

29 ♄ Saturn retrograde in Capricorn

MONDAY

30

TUESDAY

WEDNESDAY

THURSDAY

FRIDAY

SATURDAY

SUNDAY

May 2019

MONDAY

TUESDAY

1   WEDNESDAY

2   THURSDAY

3   FRIDAY

4   ♉ Taurus new moon ●   SATURDAY

5   SUNDAY

May 2019

6 ☿ Mercury enters Taurus — MONDAY

7 — TUESDAY

8 — WEDNESDAY

9 — THURSDAY

10 — FRIDAY

11 Waxing quarter moon in Leo ◗ — SATURDAY

12 — SUNDAY

     The AstroTwins' 2019 Planetary Planner

May 2019

13   MONDAY

14   TUESDAY

15   ♀ Venus enters Taurus   WEDNESDAY
       ♂ Mars enters Cancer

16   THURSDAY

17   FRIDAY

18   ♏↗ Scorpio full moon ○   SATURDAY

19   SUNDAY

May 2019

20   MONDAY

21   ♊ Sun enters Gemini   TUESDAY
      ☿ **Mercury enters Gemini**

22   WEDNESDAY

23   THURSDAY

24   FRIDAY

25   SATURDAY

26 **Waning quarter moon in Pisces** ◑   SUNDAY

          The AstroTwins' 2019 Planetary Planner

May 2019

27   MONDAY

28   TUESDAY

29   WEDNESDAY

30   THURSDAY

31   FRIDAY

SATURDAY

SUNDAY

June 2019

MONDAY

TUESDAY

WEDNESDAY

THURSDAY

FRIDAY

1 SATURDAY

2 SUNDAY

June 2019

3 ♊ Gemini new moon ● — MONDAY

4 ☿ Mercury enters Cancer — TUESDAY

5 — WEDNESDAY

6 — THURSDAY

7 — FRIDAY

8 ♀ Venus enters Gemini — SATURDAY

9 — SUNDAY

June 2019

10   Waxing quarter moon in Virgo ◐   MONDAY

11   TUESDAY

12   WEDNESDAY

13   THURSDAY

14   FRIDAY

15   SATURDAY

16   SUNDAY

June 2019

17 ♐ Sagittarius full moon — MONDAY

18 — TUESDAY

19 — WEDNESDAY

20 — THURSDAY

21 ♋ Sun enters Cancer — FRIDAY
♆ **Neptune retrograde in Pisces**

22 — SATURDAY

23 — SUNDAY

The AstroTwins' 2019 Planetary Planner   120

June 2019

24	MONDAY
25 Waning quarter moon in Aries ◐	TUESDAY
26 ☿ Mercury enters Leo	WEDNESDAY
27	THURSDAY
28	FRIDAY
29	SATURDAY
30	SUNDAY

July 2019

1 ♂ Mars enters Leo — MONDAY

2 ♋ Cancer new moon (total solar eclipse) ● — TUESDAY

3 ♀ Venus enters Cancer — WEDNESDAY

4 THURSDAY

5 FRIDAY

6 SATURDAY

7 ☿ Mercury retrograde in Leo — SUNDAY

July 2019

8   MONDAY

9   **Waxing quarter moon in Libra ◑**   TUESDAY

10   WEDNESDAY

11   THURSDAY

12   FRIDAY

13   SATURDAY

14   SUNDAY

            The AstroTwins' 2019 Planetary Planner

July 2019

15   MONDAY

16   ♑ Capricorn full moon (partial lunar eclipse) ○   TUESDAY

17   WEDNESDAY

18   THURSDAY

19   ☿ Mercury Rx enters Cancer   FRIDAY

20   SATURDAY

21   SUNDAY

July 2019

22 ♌ Sun enters Leo	MONDAY
23	TUESDAY
24 **Waning quarter moon in Taurus** ◑	WEDNESDAY
25	THURSDAY
26	FRIDAY
27 ♀ **Venus enters Leo**	SATURDAY
28	SUNDAY

The AstroTwins' 2019 Planetary Planner

July 2019

29	MONDAY

30	TUESDAY

31 ♌ Leo new moon ● ☿ **Mercury retrograde ends**	WEDNESDAY

	THURSDAY

	FRIDAY

	SATURDAY

	SUNDAY

August 2019

MONDAY

TUESDAY

WEDNESDAY

1 THURSDAY

2 FRIDAY

3 SATURDAY

4 SUNDAY

The AstroTwins' 2019 Planetary Planner

August 2019

5 — MONDAY

6 — TUESDAY

7 Waxing quarter moon in Scorpio ☾ — WEDNESDAY

8 — THURSDAY

9 — FRIDAY

10 — SATURDAY

11 ☿ Mercury enters Leo — SUNDAY

♃ Jupiter retrograde ends

♅ Uranus retrograde in Taurus

The AstroTwins' 2019 Planetary Planner   128

August 2019

12   MONDAY

13   TUESDAY

14   WEDNESDAY

15 ♒ Aquarius full moon ○   THURSDAY

16   FRIDAY

17   SATURDAY

18 ♂ Mars enters Virgo   SUNDAY

           The AstroTwins' 2019 Planetary Planner

August 2019

19
MONDAY

20
TUESDAY

21
♀ **Venus enters Virgo**
WEDNESDAY

22
THURSDAY

23
♍ Sun in Virgo
FRIDAY

Waning quarter moon in Gemini ☽

24
SATURDAY

25
SUNDAY

130

August 2019

26 — MONDAY

27 — TUESDAY

28 — WEDNESDAY

29 ☿ **Mercury enters Virgo** — THURSDAY

30 ♍ Virgo new moon ● — FRIDAY

31 — SATURDAY

— SUNDAY

September 2019

MONDAY

TUESDAY

WEDNESDAY

THURSDAY

FRIDAY

SATURDAY

1

SUNDAY

September 2019

2 | MONDAY

3 | TUESDAY

4 | WEDNESDAY

5 **Waxing quarter moon in Sagittarius ◑** | THURSDAY

6 | FRIDAY

7 | SATURDAY

8 | SUNDAY

     The AstroTwins' 2019 Planetary Planner

September 2019

9
MONDAY

10
TUESDAY

11
WEDNESDAY

12
THURSDAY

13
FRIDAY

14
♓ Pisces full moon ○
☿ Mercury enters Libra
♀ Venus enters Libra

SATURDAY

15
SUNDAY

September 2019

16	MONDAY
17	TUESDAY
18 ♄ Saturn retrograde ends	WEDNESDAY
19	THURSDAY
20	FRIDAY
21 Waning quarter moon in Gemini ◑	SATURDAY
22	SUNDAY

         The AstroTwins' 2019 Planetary Planner

September 2019

23 ♎︎ Sun enters Libra — MONDAY

24 — TUESDAY

25 — WEDNESDAY

26 — THURSDAY

27 — FRIDAY

28 ♎︎ Libra new moon ● — SATURDAY

29 — SUNDAY

September 2019

30

MONDAY

_____

TUESDAY

_____

WEDNESDAY

_____

THURSDAY

_____

FRIDAY

_____

SATURDAY

_____

SUNDAY

 The AstroTwins' 2019 Planetary Planner

October 2019

MONDAY

1

TUESDAY

2

WEDNESDAY

3 ☿ Mercury enters Scorpio

♇ Pluto retrograde ends

THURSDAY

4 ♂ Mars enters Libra

FRIDAY

5 Waxing quarter moon in Capricorn ◐

SATURDAY

6

SUNDAY

October 2019

7   MONDAY

8   ♀ **Venus enters Scorpio**   TUESDAY

9   WEDNESDAY

10   THURSDAY

11   FRIDAY

12   SATURDAY

13   ♈ Aries full moon ○   SUNDAY

          The AstroTwins' 2019 Planetary Planner

October 2019

14 _____ MONDAY

15 _____ TUESDAY

16 _____ WEDNESDAY

17 _____ THURSDAY

18 _____ FRIDAY

19 _____ SATURDAY

20 _____ SUNDAY

October 2019

21 Waning quarter moon in Cancer ◑   MONDAY

22   TUESDAY

23 ♏ Sun enters Scorpio   WEDNESDAY

24   THURSDAY

25   FRIDAY

26   SATURDAY

27 ♏ Scorpio new moon ●   SUNDAY

The AstroTwins' 2019 Planetary Planner

October 2019

28	MONDAY
29	TUESDAY
30	WEDNESDAY
31 ☿ Mercury retrograde in Scorpio	THURSDAY
	FRIDAY
	SATURDAY
	SUNDAY

The AstroTwins' 2019 Planetary Planner   142

November 2019

	MONDAY
	TUESDAY
	WEDNESDAY
	THURSDAY
1 ♀ Venus enters Sagittarius	FRIDAY
2	SATURDAY
3	SUNDAY

     The AstroTwins' 2019 Planetary Planner

November 2019

4 Waxing quarter moon in Aquarius ☽   MONDAY

5   TUESDAY

6   WEDNESDAY

7 Waxing quarter moon in Gemini ☽   THURSDAY

8   FRIDAY

9   SATURDAY

10   SUNDAY

November 2019

11	MONDAY

12 ♉ Taurus full moon ○	TUESDAY

13	WEDNESDAY

14	THURSDAY

15	FRIDAY

16	SATURDAY

17	SUNDAY

 The AstroTwins' 2019 Planetary Planner

November 2019

18
MONDAY

19
♂ Mars enters Scorpio
Waning quarter moon in Leo ☽
TUESDAY

20
☿ Mercury retrograde ends
WEDNESDAY

21
THURSDAY

22
♐ Sun enters Sagittarius
FRIDAY

23
SATURDAY

24
SUNDAY

November 2019

25 ♀ **Venus enters Capricorn**   MONDAY

26 ♐ Sagittarius new moon ●   TUESDAY

27 ♆ Neptune retrograde ends   WEDNESDAY

28   THURSDAY

29   FRIDAY

30   SATURDAY

                                                          SUNDAY

                                       The AstroTwins' 2019 Planetary Planner

December 2019

MONDAY

TUESDAY

WEDNESDAY

THURSDAY

FRIDAY

SATURDAY

1

SUNDAY

148

December 2019

2 ♃ Jupiter enters Capricorn   MONDAY

3   TUESDAY

4 Waxing quarter moon in Pisces ◑   WEDNESDAY

5   THURSDAY

6   FRIDAY

7   SATURDAY

8   SUNDAY

December 2019

9 ☿ Mercury enters Sagittarius   MONDAY

10   TUESDAY

11   WEDNESDAY

12 ♊ Gemini full moon ○   THURSDAY

13   FRIDAY

14   SATURDAY

15   SUNDAY

December 2019

16 — MONDAY

17 — TUESDAY

18 — **Waning quarter moon in Virgo** ◑ WEDNESDAY

19 — THURSDAY

20 — ♀ **Venus enters Aquarius** FRIDAY

21 — ♑ Sun enters Capricorn SATURDAY

22 — SUNDAY

December 2019

23 ———————————————————————————————————— MONDAY

24 ———————————————————————————————————— TUESDAY

25 ———————————————————————————————————— WEDNESDAY

26 ———————————————————————————————————— THURSDAY
♑ Capricorn new moon (annular solar eclipse) ●

27 ———————————————————————————————————— FRIDAY

28 ———————————————————————————————————— SATURDAY
☿ Mercury enters Capricorn

29 ———————————————————————————————————— SUNDAY

December 2019

30   MONDAY

31   TUESDAY

WEDNESDAY

THURSDAY

FRIDAY

SATURDAY

SUNDAY

 The AstroTwins' 2019 Planetary Planner

OPHIRA & TALI EDUT

Dubbed the "astrologers to the stars," identical twin sisters Ophira and Tali Edut, known as the AstroTwins, are professional astrologers who reach millions worldwide through their spot-on predictions. Through their website, Astrostyle.com, Ophira and Tali help "bring the stars down to earth" with their unique, lifestyle-based approach to astrology.

They are the official astrologers for *ELLE* Magazine and MindBodyGreen.com. The AstroTwins have been featured by major media such as the *Good Morning America*, the *New York Times* and *People* and they've collaborated with major brands including Coach, Vogue, Nordstrom, Revlon, H&M, Urban Outfitters, Ted Baker and 1Hotels.

The sisters have read charts for celebrities including Beyoncé, Stevie Wonder, Emma Roberts, Karlie Kloss and Sting. They have appeared on Bravo's *The Real Housewives of New Jersey*, doing on-air readings for the cast. They have authored numerous print books, including *Love Zodiac*, *Shoestrology* and *Momstrology* (their #1 Amazon best-selling astrological parenting guide) and a series of self-published books, including their popular annual horoscope guides. ✷

VISIT THE ASTROTWINS AT WWW.ASTROSTYLE.COM
Follow us on social media @astrotwins